AMERICA'S
GOOD NEWS
ALMANAC

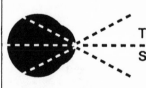 This Large Print Book carries the
Seal of Approval of N.A.V.H.

AMERICA'S GOOD NEWS ALMANAC

Inspirational True Stories
to Warm the Heart

Compiled By
Bill Bailey
"The Good News Newsman"

Thorndike Press • Thorndike, Maine

Published in 1996 by arrangement with
Pocket Books, a division of Simon & Schuster, Inc.

Thorndike Large Print ® Basic Series.

The tree indicium is a trademark of Thorndike Press.

The text of this Large Print edition is unabridged.
Other aspects of the book may vary from the original edition.

Set in 16 pt. Bookman Old Style by Rick Gundberg.

Printed in the United States on permanent paper.

Library of Congress Cataloging in Publication Data

America's good news almanac : inspirational true stories to
warm the heart / compiled by Bill Bailey.
      p.   cm.
   ISBN 0-7862-0839-2 (lg. print : hc)
   1. United States — Social life and customs — 1971– —
Anecdotes. 2. United States — Moral conditions —
Anecdotes. 3. Conduct of life —Anecdotes. 4. Large type
books. I. Bailey, Bill.
[E169.04.A529 1996]
973.92—dc20   96-30308

PERMISSIONS

CHAPTER 4

"Interview with Art Linkletter" printed with permission of Art Linkletter, TV and radio star, author, businessman.

"The Peak of His Life," by Hollis L. Engley. Courtesy Gannett News Service.

"At 93, Legal Guardian Has No Plans to Retire," by Bea Moss, *Times Herald*, August 25, 1994. Reprinted with permission of Knight-Ridder Tribune News Service.

"Bloomfield Street's Good Neighbor," by Beth Daley, *The Boston Globe*, February 3, 1995. Reprinted with permission of Knight-Ridder Tribune News Service.

"After Seven Decades, Couple Still Finds Romance in the 90s," by Clare Ansberry. Reprinted by permission of *The Wall Street Journal*, Copyright 1995, Dow Jones & Company, Inc. All Rights Reserved Worldwide.

CHAPTER 5

"Uncle Lou's Picnic," by Jerome Brond-

CHAPTER 6

CHAPTER 7

This book is dedicated to my family. They have always been the *Good News* in *my* life. My wife, Kathy, whose support for me never wavered, even in some almost impossible situations. My children, all grown now, Corrina, Colleen, Bill, and Nick, who all have positive attitudes and caring spirits. My sons-in-law, Randy and Bobby, who were lucky enough to find my daughters, and vice versa! My daughter-in-law and future daughter-in-law, Brandi and Jenel, whom my sons were lucky enough to find. My beautiful grandchildren (seven so far) Landon, Logan, Jennifer, Amanda, Chelsea, Adam, and Sarah, whose love and laughter keep me young, vital, and fresh in my perspectives, and who remind me daily of perfect love. This book and all it means to me would be nothing without them. I love you all.

ACKNOWLEDGMENTS

The idea for this book began in 1972, right after the last issue of *The Good News Paper*, which I founded and first published in 1970, was printed. *The Good News Paper*, like this book, featured the positive, inspiring stories that didn't make the headlines back during student protests, the Vietnam War, and the Charles Manson murders. Although we had over thirty thousand subscribers in fifty states, eight hundred cities, and nine foreign countries who had somehow found us without benefit of advertising or newsstand distribution, we couldn't get the advertising or working capital to keep going. We closed the paper with the knowledge that we had been successful in proving people wanted to know about the Good News going on in order to be fully informed, and also to get the full picture of the hope, heart, and heroes that represent the other side of their daily lives.

Good News became my avocation, and I continued to collect examples that should have been given prominence in the media but, as usual, were crowded out or given obscure placement to make room for the "hard" news fare of death, destruction, and doom. These past twenty-three years found me successfully publishing a local Good News paper in Southern California, which I later sold, producing a few Good News stories for television — both national and local — and digging through the media to find positive articles. Believe me, the reporters on the street find a lot of Good News, they just don't get their stories on the front page too often. My hat's off to them for their efforts at writing them so well. Especially the ones who found and wrote the stories selected for this book. They are acknowledged fully under More Acknowledgments.

While making a living as a marketing and advertising consultant, I kept working on a concept for a book of Good News. My first try, in 1984, was rejected by over a dozen publishers. But time marches on, and the parade of "bad news" continued, and a new proposal, for this book, was greeted warmly by Pocket Books Senior Editor Emily Bestler, who leads off these acknowledgments. Thanks, Emily, for having the faith in me and this book to bring it to reality . . . and give Good News a comeback!

Martha Taylor's belief in my ability and true destiny as a Good News newsman, made it possible for me to put together the proposal that sold this book to Pocket Books. Her many, many hours of work and ability to make me work made the beginning possible. Thanks, Martha, you did your job well!

The late Norman Cousins was my longtime mentor, and his wife, Ellen, provided me with a referral to New York agent Victoria Sanders, who made the sale to Pocket Books. Thanks, Ellen, and thanks, Victoria — even though you're not my agent anymore, you were there when it counted.

To Terry Dennis, my old friend and editor with me twenty-five years ago on *The Good News Newspaper*, thanks for loaning me a computer and helping me learn WordPerfect, thus bringing an old dinosaur of typewriters into the computer age.

To Diane Dean Epps, fellow writer and friend, thanks for saving me from disaster by steering me the right way when you read the first draft of my first chapter.

To Joy Doyle, for making my home office possible. Without your backing and support I would have had to write this book on a picnic table.

To Karl-Heinz Rolka and his wife, Resi, of Germany, for giving me consulting work that kept bread on the table during a very critical time. I promise you a *Germany's Good News Almanac* one day!

To Terry Pickett, whom I met in the Army in Germany in 1963 and who is now a professor at the University of Alabama and an author himself, for all the years of hearing from me about the book I was going to write about Good News. And a special thanks to his daughter, Jessica, my goddaughter, for help in rescuing my files.

To Gloria Gray, the world's greatest numerologist, and believer in all good things, for predicting this book on my birthday in 1994.

To Art Linkletter, thanks for writing an endorsement letter for my book before it was sold, and for the marvelous interview that leads off "The Old and the Bold" chapter. You are great!

To Jack Canfield, co-author of the inspiring best-seller *Chicken Soup for the Soul* for his endorsement, which is proudly displayed on the back cover.

Last, but of equal importance to acknowledge for this book, are some people who put their faith, trust, and best efforts to work many years ago to try to get Good News out sooner:

To Saul Bass, a kindred spirit who just happens to be the world's finest graphic designer, humanitarian, and creative genius, for encouraging me in 1971, and for designing a cover for a Good News book I was going to publish myself in 1984. Thanks, Saul — it's a reality now.

To Rosalie Heacock and her late husband, Jim, for being my first agents in

1983 and doing everything possible to sell my book. You were right about it. It just took eleven years for the right publisher to agree with you. Thanks, Rosalie, and thanks Jim, wherever you are in literary heaven.

To my mom and dad, who, in their lifetime, ingrained in me the persistence and courage with which they led their lives.

To all my cousins, aunts, and uncles, alive and passed on, thanks for not calling me crazy and being there for my many late night calls.

To everyone in the class of '56, who thought I'd be an actor . . . this is better!

To the God that makes us all and allows us to make all those mistakes, yet loves us just the same . . . *thank you.*

CONTENTS

17

CHAPTER 3

YOUTH IS *NOT* WASTED
ON THE YOUNG   75

CHAPTER 4

THE OLD AND THE BOLD — OUR CLASSIC CITIZENS 100

CHAPTER 5

MAKING A DIFFERENCE: CARING, SHARING AMERICANS 134

CHAPTER 6

CORPORATIONS *DO* HAVE HEARTS   196

21

CHAPTER 9

HUMOR IN THE NEWS   289

MORE ACKNOWLEDGMENTS   303

CHAPTER 1

THE GOOD NEWS
ABOUT THE BAD NEWS

If news is not really news unless it
is bad news, it may be difficult to
claim we are an informed nation.

—Norman Cousins

The complaint about too much bad
news is not a new one. In 442 B.C.
Sophocles said, "Nobody likes the
bringer of bad news." Oliver Wendell
Holmes said in 1858 that "a great calam-
ity is as old as the trilobites an hour after
it has happened." Thomas Jefferson
held the newspapers of his time in such
disdain that he once stated, "The man
who never looks into a newspaper is
better informed than he who reads
them. Inasmuch as he who knows nothing is nearer to truth than he whose
mind is filled with falsehood and errors."
Brooks Atkinson quipped in 1951 that
"the evil that men do lives on the front

pages of greedy newspapers, but the good is oft interred apathetically inside."

Television doesn't fare any better. Mike Wallace, an elder statesman of TV news, was quoted in 1995 as saying, "We're losing the confidence of the American public," while referring to a 1994 *Wall Street Journal* poll that showed only 21 percent of respondents thought the media are "honest." A Gallup poll that same year found only 35 percent of the public expressing a "great deal" of confidence in TV news.

The most persistent lament from the public, as well as media critics, is that the nation's press has "a bad news bias." As a self-proclaimed Good News Newsman, I have spent a good part of the past twenty-five years campaigning for more "Good News" coverage, beginning with my "world's first good news newspaper" in 1970, which set out to prove that there were plenty of positive stories that were either being overlooked by the mainstream media or not given prominence. *The Good News Paper* printed sixteen to thirty-two pages of only good news for almost two years, and we never had trouble finding stories.

Does the media have a "bad news

bias"? My own research has found this untrue of the majority of reporters who gather the news, as most of them attempt to find and report positive stories such as the ones you will read in this book.

What the press is guilty of is a lack of *balance* in presenting the news. Because the headlines and lead TV news stories are so often devoted to sensational accounts of crisis, controversy, crime, and conflict, it appears that the news media are interested in reporting only what's wrong about us and not interested in what's right about us.

The good news about the press is this: They *are* gathering good news stories every day. They are reporting good news stories every day. The fact that most of us have trouble finding the Good News is the fault of editors who decide to place it deep inside the front pages, often in lightly read sections of the newspaper or, in the case of TV news, to almost always ignore good news altogether. In compiling the positive news for this book, I found a majority of the selections in the mainstream media: the Associated Press wire, newspapers, newspaper syndicates, the news on the Internet, news magazines and other periodicals. But they weren't always easy to find. One story about five million young people pledging over thirty-one million hours of their time for community service was found in the "TV Notes" section of a major newspaper, I guess because the editor saw that the news release had come from *Nickelodeon*®, the kids' cable channel, which had staged a national "Help-A-Thon" designed to introduce kids to volunteerism. The sad part about this "misplacing" of a significant story is that the same paper's *front* page featured a story about two teenagers in New York killing another teenager. It is precisely this type of editorial decision making that gives the nation's press the reputation of having a bad news bias.

For every overhyped story of pop celebrity or political scandal or bloody crime, there are stories written by dedicated, talented reporters and columnists about people overcoming obstacles, heroic deeds, and solving problems — and other accounts of a positive, inspiring nature . . . in other words, Good News!

The real problem is simply that the media do not give these uplifting stories the prominence they deserve. Why don't they? I believe it is because of economics and habit.

The press knows that an O. J. murder trial, a political scandal, a natural disaster, an airplane crash, sells papers and boosts ratings. They are less sure that stories of hope, heart, and heroes will do the same. And news *is* a business — businesses need profits. This is the economic reason.

It has become a habit of the press that a solution to a problem rarely gets the amount of coverage that the problem itself was given. If a problem of national importance is given a front-page headline or lead story status in news broadcasts, and this attention succeeds in arousing the populace to go out and solve that problem, shouldn't the fact that it is solved, or attempts to solve it, also receive a front-page headline or lead story status? When the top story is about teenagers killing each other, couldn't the editors run a story alongside it about those five million teenagers who are volunteering their services to their community? I believe that is the *balanced* type of coverage of the daily news we all seek. It's not so much that we don't want to hear the bad news as we'd like to be given more good news in equal prominence with the bad. This is the "habit" of giving all the prominence to problems.

A lack of balanced news coverage can distort our perception of reality. Crime in America is a powerful example. It seems that nothing pervades the headlines and TV shows as much as crime stories. From murders, rapes, robberies, and juvenile gangs to massive coverage of murder trials to cop shows, reality-based and fiction, the media thrives on a seemingly endless marathon of sensationalistic accounts of crime in America. Crime lends itself to dramatic TV, graphic photos, and chilling, terrifying journalism. "If it bleeds, it leads," is the motto of a majority of news organizations. A national commission on violence of the sixties described the nation's fear of crime this way: "To millions of Americans few things are more pervasive, more frightening, more real today than violent crime . . . The fear of being victimized by criminal attack has touched us all in some new way."

Today, if we believe the news, we are in even more danger than ever before of being a victim of violence in our homes and on our streets.

But the dominance of crime in the news does not always reflect the reality of actual crime statistics. By sensation-alizing crime, the media actually distort what is really happening. Overcoverage leads us to believe that things are getting worse, even when the opposite is true.

Most Americans believe that serious crime has increased dramatically over the last few years. They are wrong. Serious crimes reported to police actually *dropped* 3 percent in 1992, 1993, and 1994, according to the FBI, with *double-digit decreases* in some cities, including (surprise) Los Angeles, with a 12 percent drop in overall crime.

The nation's murder rate does *not* escalate every year. In fact, it *dropped* 9 percent between 1980 and 1992, and for the first six months of 1995 — with New York City heading toward a twenty-five-year low in killings, L.A.'s murder rate down 33 percent, and Houston's homicide rate dropping 47.9 percent since 1991, the trend clearly is toward a *reduction* in homicides nationally. The peak periods for homicide rates in this century did not come this year or last, but in 1931 to 1934 and 1979 to 1981.

Homicides accounted for approximately 25,500 deaths in 1994, which is a tragedy, but in the ten leading causes of death of Americans, murder ranks dead last, at number ten behind suicide, AIDS, diabetes, pneumonia and influenza, accidents, lung disease, stroke, cancer, and heart disease, which ranks number one. Much of the material and statistical data that appears in this chapter was researched and written about by David Zucchino of Knight-Ridder News Service in a timely November 1994 article titled "Today's Violent Crime Is an Old Story with a Twist." We gratefully acknowledge his efforts.

Most of us would certainly believe that crime victimization rates have reached record levels. They have. They are at their *lowest levels in twenty years.*

How about aggravated assault and robbery? Surely these must be higher than ever. We can't pick up a paper without reading about those crimes. Actually, *both dropped 11 percent between 1973 and 1992.*

All of the headlines about drive-by shootings, drug-related gunfire, and holdups might lead us to think these events are to blame for most shooting deaths . . . but this is not even close to the truth. The most common shooting death in America takes place not on the street, but in the home . . . by suicide. There are more suicides than homicides every year.

How about juvenile crime? "The use of guns by young males of all races — rather than a rise in the number of violent acts each one commits — has created a distorted perception of a nation beset by random juvenile violence," according to Jeffrey A. Roth, co-editor of a four-volume study by the National Research Council titled *Understanding and Preventing Violence.*

The victimization surgery, by the Bureau of Justice Statistics, is regarded by many criminologists as a better gauge of crime than police reports because the survey asks people if they have been crime victims not whether or not they told the police.

In case you missed this report on your front pages, the 1992 survey found that crimes against all Americans *fell by more than 5 percent.* In all, there were *two million fewer crimes* in 1992 than in 1991, and the estimated number of crimes in 1992 was *almost eight million lower* than in 1979, despite population increases.

New Yorkers can take heart . . . in 1992, the burglary rate in London was twice that of New York.

Of course we all know that statistics can be gathered that support the contention that there is more crime today than ever before, but the overwhelming statistical data supports the facts that overall crime has gone down, except for occasional waves, consistently, decade after decade. A look at historical records proves we are living in a far safer world today than we were a hundred years ago, and we will be living in a safer world a hundred years from now than today.

I chose the data on crime only because it is one of the issues covered by the media that causes most of us the greatest fear and anxiety.

While all these drops in crimes were taking place, very little of this significant story was reflected in newspapers or TV newscasts. In fact, news coverage of violent crime by the three major networks *doubled* from 1992 to 1993, according to a recent survey by the Center for Media and Public Affairs. And coverage of murders *tripled,* though the nation's murder rate did not change . . . and this was before the media circuses of the O. J. Simpson, Susan Smith, and Menendez brothers cases. Is it any wonder most of us are scared to death about crime?

Local TV news was as guilty as the networks in their overhype of crime stories. Rocky Mountain Media Watch Group, founded by Paul Klite, a Denver physician, surveyed local newscasts on fifty TV stations in twenty-nine cities across the nation for one night on January 11, 1995. The survey showed that crime stories were the most frequently occurring topic. Fifty-seven percent were local items; 42 percent were national.

Every city seemed to have its own grisly local example of inhumanity: son shoots mother five times with bow and arrow (Pittsburgh), boyfriend sets girlfriend on fire (Chicago), body mutilated and put on display (Austin), just to name a few.

The survey revealed that the most crime news was reported by a station in Austin, Texas, with 83.1 percent of its program devoted to it; a station in Atlanta, with 70.7 percent, and a station in Washington, D.C., with 55.2 percent. For all fifty stations the average percent of news time devoted to crime was 28.5 percent, with the majority (53 percent) about murder. Adding disasters and war stories into the coverage, the "big three" of crime, war, and disasters averaged 53 to 70 percent of total news programming of the stations, the survey found.

"Most of us have the sense that crime has been moving up incessantly," said Alfred Blumstein, a criminologist at Carnegie-Mellon University. "That's because a crime-increase story is a page one story and a crime-decrease story is a page twenty-three story."

One of the arguments the press always gives when challenged about the overabundance of violent news stories is "We are just giving the public what they want." But a special ABC News *Viewpoint* poll doesn't support that statement.

The poll showed that 54 percent of Americans felt that "television news gives stories about violent crimes too much attention," and 82 percent agreed with the statement that "TV news stories about violence have made Americans more fearful than they were in the days before there was television."

Of significance to this Good News Newsman, and the readers of this book, 77 percent of those polled said that "TV news should run more stories about good news and fewer stories about violence."

Public opinion polls reflect the same desire for more good news in our newspapers as well. You might well ask, "How do we get the press to listen?" You can let your newspaper editors and TV news producers know what stories you like or dislike in the news. Believe me, they will listen. As I stated earlier, news is a business. And businesses respond to their customers. Talk it up, with phone calls and letters. You're the customer, and if you demand more balanced coverage of the news, you will get it. Remember, the ultimate "censor" of the news media is ratings and circulation. You, the viewer and reader have the power. Use it!

Meanwhile, I hope you will turn to the stories in this book for your daily dose of "positive sensationalism." These stories are important entries in the asset side of America's balance sheet. Consider *America's Good News Almanac* an antidote to what ails you, particularly if you're ailing from an overdose of bad news.

The people you will read about here will inspire you, amaze you, and make you want to meet them. They are honest, courageous, and tenacious, and they possess the hope and heart that personify the ideals of people everywhere. They illustrate through their actions that the basic virtues many assert are slipping away are, in fact, alive and well. They are real-life role models of ordinary people doing extraordinary acts. Savor their stories, use them to counteract the negative perceptions that may be inflicted upon you by the media, and by all means, use them as encouragement for your own efforts to be a good news advocate who seeks out the positive side of life. The stories selected for this first book of *America's Good News Almanac* are only the tip of the iceberg. I invite you, the readers, to send me your good news stories for consideration for the next edition. If your story is used, you will receive acknowledgment in the book, as well as an autographed copy of the edition it appears in. Send your stories to: Bill Bailey, The Good News Newsman, 4363 Hazel Avenue, Suite 1234, Fair Oaks, CA 95628.

CHAPTER 2

HEROES
OF ALL KINDS

It's the action, not the fruit of the
action, that's important. You have
to do the right thing. It may not be
in your power, may not be in your
time, that there'll be any fruit. But
that doesn't mean you stop doing
the right thing. You may never know
what results come from your action.
But if you do nothing, there will be
no result.

—Gandhi

Introduction

It is said that we live in an antiheroic
time. It is a commonplace, almost a
cliche, that the unselfish America of the
Statue of Liberty has become the Land
of Me — that the old values of personal
courage and public concern that once
helped define us to ourselves and to the

world have grown rusty from disuse. Our official heroes have too often been spoiled for us by officeholders corrupted by power, by athletes and entertainers drunk on drugs and money, by space shots that no longer seem to work. We have been told, more than once, that there ARE no heroes anymore.

And yet we live surrounded by evidence that there are — that America is still, in the words of one of its favorite anthems, the home of the brave. A selection of latter-day heroes walk the pages that follow, men, women and children whose deeds of bravery, will and self-sacrifice have made us better as a people. They are, for the most part, heroes of everyday life, as various as the American people and as ordinary to look at as the neighbors next door. They are unencumbered by medals and gold braid and unsung beyond their local papers. They tend to reject the very word hero when it is put to them; the term has a trace of old-world grandiosity to American ears, and, except in wartime or on the sports pages, we are uncomfortable with it.

But heroes are what they are, if heroism has to do with a can-do spirit in the face of long odds, great danger, hard personal adversity and crying public need. Some have risked death to save others. Some have triumphed over crippling injury and illness, others over the disabilities of sex, color, caste, poverty and age. Some have devoted their own lives and meager fortunes to reducing the sum of suffering in the world, feeding the hungry, sheltering the homeless, comforting the sick and aged; they bear daily witness to Camus's observation that plagues help human beings rise above themselves.

They are heirs to an ethos as old as the nation itself. The values they embody are by no means uniquely American. But crossing 3,000 miles of ocean to get there was itself an act of courage, repeated tens of millions of times, and settling a wilderness demanded both individual effort and neighborly concern for our first families to survive.

That those traits endure among us is plain in the stories here — stories of a woman in California, horribly burned, who saved a family from fire; a man in South Carolina who gives practically everything he earns to the poor; a Judge in Atlanta whose unpaid talents as a paramedic have saved hundreds of lives — They are parables for a pinched time- exemplary tales that remind us what we still can be.

◆ ◆ ◆

Death by fire is one of our deepest fears. Burn victims who survive their injuries say that even the flame of a candle reignites their horror. So it was for RaNelle Wallace when one winter morning she faced for a second time her mortal enemy — fire.

"I'm Going to Die!"

Bakersfield, California

Terry and RaNelle Wallace were flying home from a job-hunting trip in Utah one day in 1985 when a mountainous storm overtook their Beach Bonanza in the mountains. The sky closed around them, black and ugly, and all Terry could see over his controls were walls of rock looming in the fog. They were boxed in a valley, and when they tried to follow a road leading out, the plane hit a mountain. The Wallaces got free, but the gas tank exploded and bathed them in flame.

RaNelle, now 34, remembers sitting dazed on a boulder for a time, letting the rain cool the burns covering three-quarters of her body; her husband was somewhere nearby, his hands charred and useless. In spite of their injuries they were forced to seek help for themselves, so they started down the mountain in the fog.

They found a highway and signaled for help, two figures out of a hellscape by Bosch waving at the cars going by. More than 30 sped past before a trucker picked them up. RaNelle glimpsed her reflection in the grille. She had been beautiful once, a TV reporter, but what was left of her blond hair was black and brittle, and her face had melted into formless flesh. The woman staring back at her was a MONSTER. She started screaming.

RaNelle's nightmare had only begun. Her treatment was long and painful, her reconstruction incomplete; when she came home for Christmas, Jason, her two-year-old, shrieked and ran away. She had to use a stocking mask for a time to protect her face. While she wore the stocking, she was repeatedly mistaken for a robber; once a fast-food merchant handcuffed her to a pole and called the police. She was paralyzed with fear by the mere sight of fire — even a candle glowing on a dining table.

Early one February morning RaNelle looked out her bedroom window and saw smoke curling upward from a neighbor's house. She dashed outside. The house and garage were ablaze. Before she could think about what she was doing, she ran across the fields and empty lots until she got there. It was at that point that she came face to face with her terror. She peered into the garage. The door crashed shut behind her, gashing one of her hands and trapping her inside the flames. I'M GOING TO DIE, she was thinking, but the fear had left her; there was only the memory of the cars passing her on the road and the sense that she could not let someone else endure what she had. She screamed and pounded on the cars in the garage until

43

she had awakened the couple inside. Then she kicked the garage door open, ran out front and helped carry their children to safety. Only then, after her nightmare was over, did she fall into her neighbor's arms and cry.

♦ ♦ ♦

A home of our own — the American dream. For Sadie Waterford Jones, the dream was not for a home of her own, but a home for girls who had never had one. This is the story of one remarkable woman's determination to build a house and rebuild young lives.

A Home at Last!

Crestwood, Illinois

When Sadie Waterford Jones set out to build a home for African-American girls in trouble, she knew exactly what she wanted: something NICE, nicer than the neglected ones they came from, nicer than the blight of their daily lives. White girls already had that, as Mrs. Jones knew from having worked in Chicago's juvenile courts; white girls were sent to residential centers, African-American girls to reform school. So she got 20 volunteers together and started raising money to finance a center for blacks. "It never occurred to me that I couldn't do it," she says. "I just had no idea that it was going to take so long."

It took 30 years, but Mrs. Jones, twice widowed and independent of spirit, was stubborn about her vision. She believed that a pretty place to live in could be the beginning of self-esteem for an abused, neglected or delinquent child. A women's group offered her $15,000 toward an old building then on the market. She said no. "You hear too often that everything black people have is second class," she said. "I do not intend to put these girls in a second-class house. I intend to have a building built just for them."

Her insistence cost her time and money; she was 53 when she began raising money; she was 83 when construction finally started. The Sadie Waterford

Manor opened in suburban Crestwood in 1974 and it WAS nice — a handsome two-story brick house with columns out front and private cheerful rooms for each of its first 14 residents. Its program includes school, work, counseling and love.

Sadie Watertord Jones passed away in 1986 at the age of 96. This strong-willed, compassionate woman lived to see that it was not the building of the home itself that mattered, but the rebuilding of lives within the home.

♦ ♦ ♦

More than eighty thousand of America's children run away from home every month. Most eventually return on their own, but thousands find themselves trapped in a strange city with no money and no way back. Many never would have made it home until a New Jersey police chief decided to do something about a national problem.

A Free Ticket Home
for Runaway Kids

Bridgewater Township, New Jersey

For the over one million American children who run away from home every year, getting back can be the hard part — but almost forty thousand have made it because a Bridgewater Township police chief named Richard Voorhees had a stab of conscience one day in 1984. The source of the twinge was a bitter speech by the father of a boy who had been kidnapped and murdered; a special measure of the father's anger was aimed at the police for routinely telling parents in his situation to sit tight to see if their kids come home before filing a report. In fact, most do return home. But Voorhees, now fifty-six, knew from his own quarter century on the job that the complaint had merit — that the police too frequently *do* assume that a child can find his or her own way in from the cold.

Voorhees went back to the station house that night with an idea. It was true that kids who leave home most often want to go back, but the fare home can be a fortune to a child on the run.

Voorhees's solution was simple; he began writing bus companies, proposing free return trips for runaways who end up in strange towns with no money and no way to earn any except through illicit activity on the street. Trailways bus company bought the idea, and in June 1984, Operation: Home Free was born; Greyhound acquired Trailways a few years ago, and expanded the Home Free program in cooperation with The International Association of Chiefs of Police. Free rides home for children between the ages of twelve and seventeen are available from any of Greyhound's twelve thousand locations nationwide, and an additional program, Let's Find Them, allows parents to travel free to pick up missing or abducted children. Thanks to a cop's act of conscience, a child who checks in with the police and checks out as a missing person can get a ride home on the house.

◆ ◆ ◆

Over five hundred thousand Americans have a devastating, crippling disease called multiple sclerosis. Deborah McKeithan is one of them. She spent her adolescence in and out of hospitals and missed so much school her dream of becoming a doctor was crushed under the weight of her disease. Deborah simply altered her goal and decided to become a nurse. That way she could still work with the terminally ill. But a stroke prevented her completion of nursing school. Nonetheless, despite the setbacks and the many times she was told "you can't," Deborah proved she could — and she changed the lives of millions of disabled persons in the process.

Don't Tell Deborah What Can't Be Done!

Charlotte, North Carolina

Life began again for Deborah McKeithan the day she entered a wheelchair beauty pageant in 1978 and discovered just how tough she was. She had been stricken in her teens by multiple sclerosis and epilepsy and had recovered enough to nearly complete nursing school only to suffer a disabling stroke. She couldn't even speak intelligibly, but her will was intact, and she practiced in front of a mirror every day until she could talk again. On the night of the Miss Wheelchair Pageant of North Carolina, Deborah gave a speech about making a life for herself through helping others. She won first runner-up.

Before Deborah was able to act on her plans, however, she had another serious episode and her MS was deemed uncontrollable. Her doctors believed there was nothing more they could do for her. So for the fourth time in her life, Deborah was told she wouldn't live much longer. She was only twenty-four years old.

Deborah wouldn't accept the doctors' verdict. She learned that experimental treatments for MS were being conducted at Methodist Hospital in Houston and she got herself admitted. She was given medications once labeled "too aggressive" — but they worked! They kept her brain from swelling and helped control her seizures. She went home, and not in a wheelchair either. With the help of a cane, she walked once again.

For the first time in many years, Deborah finally had the energy to do something. She wasn't about to waste it. "Who you were before you became disabled is who you will be afterward," she had learned. "Life," she says, "can have two purposes: an *excuse from or a rea-*

son for. Some people look for an excuse not to be living and when they are handed a disability, they're happy; now they have a professional 'gonna do,' " Deborah says. " 'I was gonna do that' is unspoken but acknowledged. Or," she continues, "life becomes a reason for, and those are the ones you find within the disabled community educating and changing the world."

Deborah's "reason for" became apparent when she returned to Charlotte and rallied her friends and supporters to form the country's first chapter of HOW — Handicapped Organized Women — with the motto "Help ourselves by helping others."

HOW took on such diverse tasks as gathering clothing for refugee children, visiting newly disabled people at home and in hospitals, and making service calls to the elderly.

Her new organization hit the national news. Major newspapers in New York printed several interviews with her. "It wasn't expected," Deborah says. "It's not normal for a disabled person to help others, because others are typically wanting to help them." Sally Jessy Raphaël was so impressed she had Deborah on her talk show twice and then signed on as a HOW board member.

Soon, disabled men were wanting to join HOW. Deborah told them jokingly that they were invited only when they put on dresses and shaved. The next meeting, three men arrived in dresses and clean-shaven . . . even their legs. The following week HIM — Handicapped Independent Men — was born. "I'm not a person who goes against my word," Deborah declares.

HOW received its first endowment when Deborah won the Endow a Dream award from Chicago's W. Clement Stone Foundation for overcoming adversity with a positive attitude. Art Linkletter, who presented the award, was so impressed with her spirit, he encouraged her to embark upon public speaking. They continue to stay in contact to this day.

Like many of the disabled in the eighties, Deborah found herself entangled in a governmental catch-22. She'd been living on Social Security and disability while turning in her paycheck from HOW to the government. If she gave up Social Security, she'd also have to give up Medicare, a necessity for any disabled person who requires medical support, because preexisting conditions make it impossible to secure coverage under many insurance plans.

The way Deborah saw it, the government was "paying" the disabled to do nothing and just deteriorate, but the "pay" was so bad, most disabled persons preferred to work.

She decided to do something about it. She drafted a letter to Ronald Reagan, who was president at the time, requesting that the disabled be allowed to purchase Medicare insurance on a sliding-scale fee. Then, if they could work successfully, they could give up Social Security payments, but still keep their health insurance.

Deborah's letter captured the President's attention and she was invited to Washington to testify on behalf of the disabled. In 1985, the Deborah McKeithan bill was passed, allowing for the first time a disabled person to enter the workforce and purchase Medicare insurance on a sliding scale. The President's commission recruited her to help draft the Americans with Disabilities Act. From a simple letter to her president, Deborah found herself working alongside senators and congressmen drafting legislation on behalf of the entire disabled community. Deborah's determination had helped millions of disabled Americans to have the opportunity of independence.

Deborah wants others to do the same. "Horses are handicapped, people are disabled," is a motto Deborah uses in her lectures. But there is more, she says: "First you are a person, you have a name, and you might just happen to be disabled." In a strange way, her long-ago dream of working with the terminally ill has adapted well to the disabled population.

"I'm telling people who are dealing with the death of their body as they knew it that they have to live, but their body as they knew it died. They must get used to this new temple, this new casing, these new *abilities*," she says. "Some people never get past it. For others, it's a springboard. Those are the people whose injustices give them a reason for making a difference."

Deborah is in her forties now and because of her MS, epilepsy, and failing eyesight, she has to have someone near her constantly. She chose a specially trained Seeing Eye dog named Carson, an oversized black Labrador. Carson knows when Deborah is safe and somehow he always knows when she's not. "It's the aura," she says. "He'll come to me as I'm blacking out, nuzzle my hand with his nose and run for help."

It was Carson who got Deborah involved in her latest cause as national spokeswoman for Guiding Eyes for the Blind. "Life is full of detours, but it can be exciting and different if you're openminded," Deborah surmises. Just don't tell Deborah McKeithan what can't be done — she's doing it!

◆ ◆ ◆

There are many stories in today's news about the disregard for human life among America's young people. This is not one of them.

Three Wrong Guys Who Had the Right Stuff

Boston, Massachusetts

They were criminals in the eyes of the law, but for a moment when it counted, Ed Comeau, Alan MacDonald and Joe

Parks were wrong guys with the right stuff. The three of them, doing time for robbery at a detention center, were playing football in a field on the frozen Muddy River one mild February day when a boy of 13 fell through the thawing ice. A cry went up. The men ran over. The boy was thrashing in the water 25 feet from the bank.

"I ain't gonna let ANYBODY die," Mac-Donald said afterward, nor as it turned out, were his pals. Comeau, 21, plunged in and found himself in trouble; the cold sapped his strength, and the boy was almost dragging him under. Parks, 27, tried to get close, but the ice gave under him, and he was in the water, too. That left MacDonald, 26, a behemoth who once interested the Miami Dolphins. He stepped out a few feet onto the frozen surface, and as Comeau and Parks struggled toward him with the boy, he dragged them out one by one.

The three were up for parole, and their good deed sped the paperwork: they were out the next summer. Some jail mates traded cynical jokes about throwing kids in the river so they could get sprung too. But James Miller, the boy they saved, wasn't examining motives.

"These three dudes came along and pulled me out," he said. "They're all right."

♦ ♦ ♦

John Fling calls himself "just an ordinary guy." He's not rich — he lives on his retirement from a blue-collar job and Social Security. And he has had a hobby, for over forty-eight years — helping people. At age seventy-two, John spends most of his waking hours giving everything he has to helping those in need.

The Saint of South Carolina

Columbia, South Carolina

One of nineteen children, John Fling grew up in Gabbettville, Georgia (population, forty-six). His parents were so poor they weren't even sharecroppers; they were sharecroppers' helpers. What family members ate, they had to catch out of the water, dig out of the ground, or shake out of a tree. At age twelve, John quit school to work in the cotton fields, where he labored for six years.

At age twenty-five, after a six-year stint in the U.S. Army, John settled with his wife in Columbia, South Carolina, landing a job as supervisor to a hundred boys who delivered newspapers. He began providing them and their families with food, clothing, and school supplies. Helping others became his personal mission.

One night in 1951, John accompanied the police to settle a domestic dispute. The couple had a small baby, but apparently the boy wasn't fathered by the woman's husband. John asked if it would solve the problem if he took the baby. The couple readily agreed, signing a scrap of paper that gave John all rights to the baby. John and his wife, Jane, raised the child along with their natural son.

John and his wife never owned a home. They now live on Social Security, in a rent-free cottage behind his mother-in-law's house. Though he has worked all his life — sometimes several jobs at once — John is without almost any material possessions. Before he retired as a parts deliveryman, John's employer, Love Chevrolet, gave him clothes to wear and a truck to drive, and lots of time to pursue his hobby — helping people.

The clothing John gives away is often better than what he wears. He hasn't bought clothes, except underwear for over twenty years. He doesn't have a television, or the time to look at one. Only recently did John get a telephone — to better serve those who depend on him. He has never owned a car, but he has bought cars for five others.

For over forty-seven years, John Fling has spent most of his waking hours driving the streets of Columbia, looking for someone he can help. There has not been a single day that he hasn't done something to help the poor. He delivers food, medicine, and laundry, helps with bills, repairs screen doors, mows lawns, unstops sinks, transports the needy to appointments — for an extended family that includes forty blind people, two hundred seniors, and four hundred children.

Having lost the sight in one eye in a boyhood hunting accident, John shows a special interest in the blind. He gives them rides and takes them to the beach or fishing. He drives his more adventurous blind friends out to a cow pasture, settles them into a go-cart, places earphones on their heads, sits on his truck, and, using a two-way radio, tells them to go left or right. Some of them are "hot rods."

John is caring, selfless, and limitless in energy. He is unincorporated and refuses to become a nonprofit organization. There is no board to direct him, no committee to support his activities. Most of the money he hands out is donated by local businesspeople and by friends around the country. He often takes the last dime out of his own pocket to help someone.

Once while visiting a nursing home with two deacons from his church, John met an elderly woman who said she didn't know what time to take her medicine because she didn't have a watch. John pulled the watch from his own wrist, handed it to the woman, and walked on. That is typical charity, John Fling style.

As the three men left the nursing home, John met a one-legged man on the street who said he needed a raincoat. John took off his own coat and gave it to the man. One of the deacons said to John, "Let's get back in the truck before you give away your pants."

John's first love is still the children. As he drives through Columbia's back alleys, kids emerge from the shadows and rush the truck. Embracing as many as he can, John asks them how they are and what they need, and gives them what he can. As he leaves, John comments to a visitor, "Even more than money, what they need most is love."

And John gives them lots of love.

At five-thirty A.M. every Sunday, John starts driving a donated van three hours to go to the Baptist church in the next town, collecting as many as seventy-nine children as he travels a fifty-five-mile round-trip. On the way home, he stops at a restaurant and treats each of the children to a meal.

Every Christmas, John provides the kids he cares for a shopping spree at one of the local department stores. One year, he took 1,216 children to Kmart, providing them each with a fifty-dollar gift certificate. To encourage kids to take their education seriously, he offers twenty dollars to students making B's and higher on their report cards. Grades have soared.

Over the years, John's generosity has become known throughout the world. When a man in India wrote to a man he knew only as "John Fling, USA," to request help in obtaining a prosthesis, and the letter somehow arrived, John's response was equally characteristic. Somehow he found the money to buy and send the needed prosthesis.

John Fling has received countless awards for his selfless efforts, including being selected one of six recipients of the 1991 America's Awards. Instituted by the Norman Vincent Peale Foundation, it honors unsung heroes who personify the American character and spirit. America's Awards have been hailed by the Washington news media as "the Nobel Prize for Goodness."

Although John is now in his seventies, he continues to have a tremendous impact in his role as a one-man social service agency. Few people in South Carolina are as well known and few people in the world are as well loved. When you ask about John Fling, the first thing people say, more often than not, is "That man is a living saint."

(Author's Note: If you would like to help

John Fling, the address is: John Fling Ministries, P.O. Box 5491, West Columbia-Cayce, SC 29171.)

◆ ◆ ◆

As a municipal court judge in Atlanta, Arthur Kaplan often has to observe the hopelessness of a life that can't be saved. But nights and weekends, it's a different story.

"Rescue 10" — The Heart Behind the Gavel

Atlanta, Georgia

A man lay sprawled on a downtown sidewalk, his throat cut ear to ear, an artery spurting blood. A lone policeman was trying to stop the geyser with a towel when a familiar figure churned through the crowd, a man in his sixties in a white medic's coat with RESCUE in red letters on the back. He took charge, stopped the bleeding, saw to the necessary measures against shock, and waved the man off by ambulance to Grady Hospital — one of over twenty-four thousand street casualties Arthur M. Kaplan has tended in nearly thirty-eight years as a one-man rescue squad.

By day, he is a part-time judge of the municipal court. But nights and weekends, he goes by the radio handle "Rescue 10," bringing help to the victims of auto crashes and violent crimes.

Judge Kaplan came by his avocation when, as a Red Cross trainer in first aid, he saw a couple lying dead of injuries sustained in a wreck because no one had known what to do for them. Soon after, Kaplan put a police radio in his car and began responding to calls, bringing bandages, splints, and know-how. He has even been shot at, and on one occasion he found himself shooting back at the gunman waging a firefight with a cop. He wound up treating both men for multiple bullet wounds. The gunman wrote from prison, thanking him for saving so unworthy a life. To Judge Kaplan, now sixty-eight, *any* life is worth saving, and if he gets there in time, he says, he will save it.

During the past thirty years Judge Kaplan has personally trained over fifteen thousand individuals in Emergency Medical and Red Cross First Aid courses, including EMTs, nurses, physicians, FBI agents, Secret Service agents, and law enforcement personnel in Georgia and throughout the United States. Judge Kaplan is the recipient of more American National Red Cross Certificates of Merit for Lifesaving than any other individual in the country.

The Judge has never received compensation for his contributions to emergency medical care and his rescue efforts. He pays for his own car, gas, and expenses so as not to be a burden to anybody.

He sums it up by saying, "There's a certain feeling of gratification to match wits with fate and outwit it. One of the most beautiful things in the world is to see someone breathe again. They don't have to speak to say thank you. They say it with their eyes when they look up at you."

◆ ◆ ◆

It was 1933, in the middle of the Great Depression, when the Children's Center in Houston came to Clyde and Pauline Waldrop's door with a baby no one wanted. In those days, if no foster home could be found, unwanted babies were institutionalized. Would they take

65

the baby in until adoptive parents could be found? The Waldrops, childless themselves, did — and so began a career in parenting that was to last for over fifty years.

Counting the Blessings of Motherhood

Houston, Texas

"It is a blessing to be a mother and have a child," says Pauline Waldrop, eighty-eight, and she should know; until her retirement from parenting in 1984, she had 726 of them. She and her husband, Clyde, childless themselves, took in their first foster son in 1933, when he was only ten days old, and wept when he left at ten months. The only way to ease the pain of losing one, they found, was to bring home another, and another, and another — a chain that continued through Clyde's death in 1942 and now spans over a half century. "I never intended to do it all those years," Mrs. Waldrop says. "Time passes. I just got started and couldn't stop. Those babies had no mommies or daddies. They needed love, not institutions — we just wanted to give them a chance."

Pauline's brood came in all sizes, shapes, colors, and states of health. Some were black, and many were handicapped, from that first baby, who had a cleft palate, to another with club feet who grew up to become a doctor, and the last, an infant girl with cerebral palsy. "We took any of 'em," Mrs. Waldrop remembers. She got to mother only two all the way to adulthood — Richard Beasley now fifty-one, and Ellis Duff, now fifty-three — but she loved them all as if they were her own. The Waldrops were plain people, and the support money from the Children's Center never quite covered the bills. They didn't even have a telephone when they began. Sometimes the social worker from the center would appear at the door unannounced with a new child.

The Waldrops never said no, taking in up to six at a time. Pauline Waldrop lives by herself now. Numerous awards for her public service line the walls — the Jefferson Award, the Sertoma International Service to Mankind Award, and many others. But the pictures of her "kids" are her most prized possessions. Those and the memories give warmth and comfort to a lady who can truly "count her blessings" — all 726 of them.

♦ ♦ ♦

They suffered the most heartbreaking sorrow — their young son's life had been suddenly taken. Yet, in the midst of their overpowering grief they were still able to give.

From Tragedy — A Gift of Life

Bodega Bay, California

Reginald and Maggie Green and their two children, Nicholas, seven, and Eleanor, four, were vacationing in Italy in the fall of 1994. They were driving along a stretch of roadway in the southern Italian region of Calabria heading for Sicily when armed and masked robbers approached their car and began harassing them. "I felt that with that recklessness and with that degree of violence in their voices that we'd be at their mercy," Reginald, who drove the car, recalled.

He tried to outrun the bandits, who gave chase and then opened fire. The Greens were able to escape but Nicholas, who was in the back seat with his sister Eleanor, was hit by a bullet. Police helped the Greens take Nicholas to the hospital.

"The bullet was lodged so deep that right from the beginning there was very little chance that he would recover," Mr. Green said. "He was being kept alive with life support and his tiny heart was gone." The doctors declared Nicholas brain dead and his parents decided, despite their desperate grief, to donate his organs.

His heart, liver, pancreas, and kidneys were in immediate demand because Italy has one of Europe's lowest rates of organ donation. "It was the easiest big decision I've ever had to make in my life," said the boy's father. "There was something magical about Nicholas. We, of course, expected a wonderful future for him. Now that he doesn't have that future, somebody else should have a chance at that kind of future."

Shortly after his death, Nicholas's organs were flown three hundred miles from Sicily to hospitals in Rome. His heart was given to a fifteen-year-old boy whose heart problems since birth had stunted his growth. Nicholas's pancreas went to a diabetic patient in Perugia.

His liver was donated to a nineteen-year-old Sicilian woman and his kidneys went to two other children. "I'd like to tell him and his parents thanks," eleven-year-old Tino Motta told reporters from his hospital bed in Catania shortly before going into surgery to receive one of Nicholas's kidneys. Motta had been on dialysis for a year.

Italy's officialdom honored the parents from Bodega Bay, California, with everything from front-page editorials in papers across the country to honorary citizenships, a gold medal from Rome, and a meeting with the premier and president. As well as reaching out to the couple, Italians looked inward.

The donation of Nicholas's organs was "a gesture of great civility that not only saved five lives, but has made Italy reflect not a little," Messina Mayor France Providenti said.

"I must, I want, to thank you; not only for the transplants, but for a lesson. Of generosity, of composure," wrote Enzo Biagi, Italy's most respected commentator, in an open letter on the front page of the Milan daily, *Corriere della Sera.* Biagi said that American values are often dismissed as naive by Italians,

"who by now hardly have faith in anything. However, every once in a while we
discover that your customs, your upbringing are not just talk, and truly you
believe in feelings."

Reginald Green remembered his son's
warmth and intellect as he spoke of
Nicolas's fascination with Greek and Roman mythology and history. "He com-
bined an innocent, trusting, and
generous nature with real intellectual
strength. He was remarkable for a boy
of his age."

His father said Nicholas's favorite
among the characters of Roman mythology was Mercury, the light-footed mes-
senger of the gods. "The idea of the small
figure doing important things, I think,
appealed to him."

◆ ◆ ◆

*In February of 1994, the tragic para-
chuting accident that cost Sergeant First
Class Dana Bowman both his legs and
took the life of his buddy made the national news. But the story that ran in the
Associated Press less than nine months
later was truly one of turning tragedy to
triumph.*

Paratrooper Loses Legs — Jumps Again!

Fort Bragg, North Carolina

A soldier who lost both legs in a parachuting accident astounded even the most gung-ho of the gung-ho when he re-enlisted for active duty, then jumped out of a plane again.

Sgt. 1st Class Dana Bowman took his oath in a yellow and black airplane belonging to the Golden Knights parachute team at the base that is home to the Army's elite 82nd Airborne Division and the Special Forces, known as the Green Berets.

Then the 32-year-old from North Ridgeville, Ohio, shoved himself out the door, 10,000 feet up, and followed his comrades to the ground, only a little less than nine months after losing his legs in the accident that left a friend dead.

When Bowman landed, the wind ruffled his pants, exposing his metal artificial legs.

"Well, I did it," Bowman said after receiving kudos from a colonel and a three-star general at a ceremony. "I'm just glad to be here standing on my feet."

Bowman is the first double amputee to

re-enlist and remain on active duty in the U.S. military, said Lt. Gen. Hugh Shelton, commander of the 18th Airborne Corps.

He's shown the "never-say-quit attitude that makes world-class athletes and world-class soldiers," Shelton said.

Soldiers of all ranks, wearing camouflage or their dress green uniforms with berets, lined up to shake Bowman's hand.

Bowman was eligible for 100 percent disability and could have quit the Army he'd served for 13 years and drawn monthly checks for the rest of his life, Shelton said.

Instead, he made his first jump just 188 days after his accident, astounding doctors and parachutists.

On February 6, 1994, Bowman, a former member of the 82nd Airborne and the Green Berets, collided in the air at more than 100 mph with partner and buddy Sgt. Jose Aquillon. Bowman's legs were severed, one above the knee and one below. Aquillon died of a heart attack after landing in a tree.

"They told me at the beginning it would be six weeks before I would get off my crutches," Bowman said. "It took me four days to get off my crutches. It took me a week to get off my cane . . . If I fall, I fall. I've had some good ones too. I broke a lot of (artificial) legs."

—Reprinted with permission of Associated Press.

CHAPTER 3

YOUTH IS *NOT* WASTED ON THE YOUNG

The youth of a nation are the trustees of posterity.

—Benjamin Disraeli

The Sacramento Bee *invites teenagers from area high schools to express their views in a weekly feature. The following essay, written by Jeffrey Alan Kukral, a student at Foothill High School, is an appropriate introduction to this chapter.*

Most Teenagers Aren't Violent or Drugged Out — But You Wouldn't Know That by Watching TV

Sacramento, California

Have you noticed that on the news at night all you see that is associated with teenagers is senseless violence, killings and such? Well I have, and I am getting sick of it.

These "bad" teens are giving the rest of us a rotten name. Why? Most of us have not done real bad things that get major coverage. Yet when I take my girlfriend out on a date or go out with my friends, we are watched with a sharp eye or interrogated as to every move we make. I have lived a good clean life. I have never owned a gun, assaulted a girl or swarmed a corner store.

There are many other teenage students like me. You know, the teens that just want to have fun without spoiling it for others. We're the ones who do our best at school, work in the community and try hard at life. Yet we don't get the attention.

The juveniles who do bad things are going to keep grabbing the spotlight if the adult world does not stop pampering them and giving them the attention. The attention is what these kids really want. It makes their day if they get a spot on the 11 P.M. news. They know from experience that they won't be punished. Maybe they'll be put in "the hall" for a couple of weeks, an experience that's like a vacation for them.

The situation could become drastic in the next few years. We might fall off the edge and never be able to climb back. But if we start giving the right people the right recognition and truly punishing those who deserve it, just possibly the "good kids" will start taking back their right to walk with some dignity and not feel like they are always on trial. Let's open up the people's ears to the goodness of teens, and make them hear us.

—By Jeffrey Kukral

Just as the preceding essay by the Sacramento teenager reflects the thinking of millions of high school students, the following story, compiled from a story by David Boldt, a reporter for the Philadelphia Inquirer, *examines a college student's new view of the world. An interview with Mr. Boldt confirmed that this:*

Ivy League Student Leader Proposes Radical Revolution: *Community!*

The warm ovation for Secretary of Health and Human Services Donna Shalala had just subsided. All that remained of Dartmouth College's convocation program was the address by the student assembly president, a segment often noted mainly for a rich trove of treasured clichés.

But today's speech was to be something different. Something more along the lines of, well, "the story of a conversion."

"Before I begin my speech," Danielle Moore told the audience of students and faculty, "I think it's important you know the changes that have taken place in my opinion and attitudes."

She then sketched her student career. Her initial "rosy" view of the world had been darkened by the difficulties coming from being a Native American freshman at Dartmouth and from learning more about "the history and current state of my people."

All this had filled her with an anger and bitterness that had been reflected in her campaign for student assembly president last spring. She had won by running against a crowded field on what might be called a victim's rights platform.

But now, she was clearly switching agendas. "After a summer of introspection," she said, "I have been able to leave my anger behind and concentrate on the revolutionary idea of community. Separatism and segregation are no longer revolutionary. Daring to try to cross the lines of color, class, gender, sexual orientation, and religion to achieve friendships, or at least some kind of understanding, is revolutionary."

She went on to criticize the way students were immediately categorized according to race, ethnicity, gender, and so forth, and then found their lives being ruled by the "collective voice" of that subgroup. The "voice" dictated the clothes they wore, the politics they professed, the way they spoke, and even the people with whom they could associate.

What was needed was a new balance that allowed a wider range of expression. It should not be "deemed unacceptable," she said, for an African-American to have politically conservative views, or for a feminist to wear makeup. Similarly, a fraternity pledge should feel free to refuse to participate in drinking activities.

This listener was startled and amazed. This was partly because Moore's poised and eloquent speech was so unexpected. On campus to drop off a son, I had come to the convocation more or less by chance, mainly to hear Secretary of Health and Human Services Shalala.

As she noted, Moore's call for "community" is fairly radical stuff to hear on an American campus these days. The required rhetoric is more often aimed at driving people apart than at bringing them together.

This is disquieting. After all, if privileged and empowered young people can't work out a better way of living together within the sequestered sanctuary of the campus, what hope is there for the rest of us?

But my favorite thing about the speech, of course, was that I couldn't have agreed with her more. What Danielle Moore was calling for on campus is what ought to take place in America.

A couple of days later, I talked with her to find out what the reaction to her speech had been and to learn more about the introspective experience that had brought about her change of views.

The reaction, she said, had been "wonderful." Many students and professors had congratulated her; several had asked for copies of the speech. As to what had changed her views, there had been no single, crystallizing experience, though she had been annoyed by the way ideological conformity was enforced during a program for minorities she'd attended early in the summer of her freshman year.

"The word *sellout* was thrown around a lot," she said, "and that's a painful word. Too often it was applied without any real examination of the argument being made, or the validity of the supposed 'sellout's' own life experience."

But more important was a gradual realization that "my anger hadn't gotten me anywhere. It was something that alienates rather than something that makes things move forward."

◆ ◆ ◆

In October of 1994, the headlines were full of a story about two teenagers in New York who savagely executed a fourteen-year-old boy. That same weekend another group of kids were engaged in an event that should have pushed the acts of two aberrant gang members out of those headlines.

Five Million Kids Say: "I Want to Help!"

Los Angeles, California

The first weekend of October in 1994, the kids' cable channel *Nickelodeon*® launched its first Big Help campaign. The idea was to get the kids who watch *Nickelodeon*, aged six to fourteen, to call in and pledge some hours of their time to work in their own communities with other volunteer groups such as 4-H, Earth Force, Points of Light, Second Harvest, Youth Power/"Just Say No," and others.

Once the pledges were made, the next step would be to convert those volunteer hours into The Big Help Day two weeks later in the cities of Boston, Orlando, Philadelphia, San Antonio, and Santa Barbara, where the kids would be connected with volunteer opportunities.

President Clinton went on the air with a taped message. Whoopi Goldberg hosted the telethon, and other celebrities including Jonathan Taylor Thomas, of *Home Improvement*, and David Robinson, of the San Antonio Spurs, were spokespersons for the event.

A custom-designed, national toll-free

calling service capable of receiving, tabulating, and reporting millions of phone calls was set up by MCI. In addition, kids could pledge their time through America Online and Prodigy.

The phone lines and computer links were opened up. The Big Help-A-Thon began. No one could foresee the results. After all, there were no free trips being offered, no autographs, no prizes for participating — just the opportunity for young people to pledge their time to help people in their communities.

The calls poured in. The phone lines and computer links were pushed to capacity. The running total on a tote board set up to keep track of calls and number of hours pledged rose by the minute. In the first hour hundreds of thousands of kids pledged well over a million hours. By the end of the twelve-hour telethon the results astounded everyone. Nearly five million kids had pledged thirty-one million plus hours of volunteer community service.

A nine-year-old girl who volunteered said, "If nobody did anything, nothing in the world would be different. Not everyone realizes that kids can make a difference too. Some adults think we can't, but we can."

"This weekend nearly five million kids proved that they're motivated to make a difference," said Geraldine Laybourne, president of *Nickelodeon*®. "By pledging over thirty-one million hours, the message they sent is loud and clear: Kids are ready, willing, and able to help."

Nickelodeon's The Big Help is a multi-year, national grassroots campaign designed to demonstrate through tangible activities that kids can make a difference in the lives of their peers in their communities. The campaign will link kids from diverse areas and backgrounds to the common experience of helping others. It will also introduce kids to positive behaviors and role models at a time when they are developing patterns that they will continue into adolescence and adulthood. Information on The Big Help can be obtained by calling (212) 258-7080 or writing to Nickelodeon, 1515 Broadway, New York, NY 10036.

♦ ♦ ♦

When Glen Besterfield, an assistant

professor at the University of South Florida College of Engineering, was approached about a special project for his student engineers to undertake, he was uncertain about their chances for success. But he and his students couldn't resist the challenge, and the result was:

A Moving Christmas Present

Tampa, Florida

Kyle Romano was just a toddler when he came down with a rare disease called meningococcemia. It damaged his circulation and caused gangrene in his arms and legs. To save his life surgeons had to amputate his arms above the elbows and take two thirds of each of his legs. Seven years old now, he has had thirty-five operations. "It was a miracle he lived," said his father, David Romano.

Kyle's twelve friends on their cul-de-sac in the Town'n Country neighborhood of Tampa all have bicycles. Kyle has wanted a bike since he was four. The problem was, no one makes bicycles for kids with no arms or legs.

Kyle's father was determined to change that. After exhausting every hope, he turned to the University of

South Florida's engineering department and presented his case to Assistant Professor Glen Besterfield. Besterfield at first thought the idea of designing and building a bike for Kyle would be nearly impossible.

"The most important considerations were how to get power out of his body and how could we make it safe for him," Besterfield said. Kyle didn't want a motorized bike. That would be too much like his wheelchair.

Professor Besterfield took the idea for the project to his students. They were enthusiastic about it. Eleven of them worked on the project for two semesters and after many attempts, the bike was a reality.

On Christmas Day of 1994, the backward-looking bike, with two wheels in the front and one in the back, tied with a big red ribbon, was presented to Kyle Romano by the university students.

"This is the best Christmas ever," Kyle declared. "I feel like I have a driver's license because I have my bike," he said as he propelled the long three-wheeler with a rocking motion. Kyle uses the stub of his right arm to steer and stub of his left arm to shift and brake. He powers the bike by pushing his chest against a padded bar and rocking. Both the forward and backward strokes of his torso keep it rolling.

"When I take it home my friends will ask, 'What in the world is this?' I will tell them, 'My bike,'" the blond, blue-eyed youngster said after a spin on the 4½-foot contraption at the USF Tampa campus. "I think the other kids will be happy I have a bike. Not just a wheelchair, but a bike!"

Brian Corces, one of the students who worked on Kyle's bike project, said, "It's the best, most worthwhile project I've undertaken in college." He said he is glad the project got a lot of news coverage because "there have to be other kids with Kyle's needs out there, and the design is very simple — more can be made very easily just like it."

◆ ◆ ◆

A fine example of "What you sow, you shall reap."

Growing Veggies — Harvesting Self-Esteem in the 'Hood

Los Angeles, California

Straight out of South Central L.A. comes Food from the 'Hood, founded by a group of high school students who have created a business dedicated to harvesting self-esteem, business acumen, and a product line from their vegetable garden.

Their chief product is Straight out 'the Garden, a creamy Italian dressing with "kickin' taste and bump-in' packaging." (Translation: It tastes good and looks good.)

Currently available in two thousand supermarkets in twenty-three states, the low-fat, all-natural dressing was developed by a partnership formed in the ashes of the 1992 riots.

At inner-city Crenshaw High School, thirty-nine students met shortly after the '92 uprising to try to make sense out of the three days that razed a good part of their community and to change their economic future.

With help from an advertising executive and corporate advisers such as Ben & Jerry's Ice Cream, and $100,000 in grants, the students eventually assembled a very successful company.

Selling vegetables, herbs, and, beginning in 1994, salad dressing, the students put their profits into a college scholarship fund while learning how to run a business. "Most people want to come in here and tell kids what *not* to do, instead of coming in here and teaching entrepreneurial workshops and telling kids what they *can* do," said thirty-seven-year-old Melinda McMullen, who took a leave of absence from the advertising firm Chiat-Day to volunteer full-time.

They are a hard-working bunch of kids, with carefully rehearsed handshakes, eye contact, and an abundance of enthusiasm. "Check this out," said sixteen-year-old Ben Osborne. "This is our garden."

The garden is a quarter acre behind the football field. The original idea was to raise produce to sell at local farmers' markets. But the first-year profits in 1993 netted only six hundred dollars, which was awarded as scholarships to three graduates.

"We had all this lettuce," recalled McMullen, so "why not make salad dressing?" The three graduates who were awarded scholarships in June of

1994 will be sharing about seven thousand dollars, almost twelve times as much as the 1993 awards. Scholarship winners are determined by their grades and their participation in the business.

Rigid health department standards and other costs made manufacturing the dressing problematic. So Food from the 'Hood, following their marketing advisers' counsel, contracted with a manufacturer to actually make the dressing for them.

They also enlisted a distributor, a supermarket broker, and a law firm. Some were paid, others donated their services. For competitive reasons, McMullen said, total sales figures for the dressing are not given out.

"It's an exciting success story," said Mary McAboy, spokeswoman for Von's supermarkets, which has more than three hundred stores in southern California and Las Vegas, all of which carry the dressing. Von's sells about 360 bottles a week, she said. "And that is very good, considering it doesn't have any national advertising campaign."

In the fall of 1994, Prince Charles visited South Central and the students of Food from the 'Hood. In preparing for the royal visit, the students got a lesson in protocol, public speaking, and planning a media event. The prince was impressed, and the event received national press coverage.

The sky appears to be the limit for the future of Food from the 'Hood. Norris Bernstein, founder of Bernstein's salad dressing business, has offered business advice. Nissan donated a new minivan to haul the students' produce to farmers' markets. And Ben & Jerry's will offer one-dollar ice cream coupons to purchasers of Straight out 'the Garden. When these hardworking entrepreneurial students are asked one day how they got their start, they are likely to reply, "From the ground up!"

♦ ♦ ♦

Marathons attract runners from all over the globe. The grueling 26.2-mile race is considered the ultimate test of endurance and determination. To simply cross the finish line is an accomplishment for many. For Dack Axell, it was a miracle just to begin.

"I Want to Go a Little Further!"

Richmond, Virginia

David Wayne Axelle, Jr. — Dack to his friends — was born with spina bifida, a rare birth defect that left his lower body nearly useless. "He'll be a good citizen," a doctor told the boy's father, Dave, Sr. There wasn't much more he could promise Dack, beyond the prospect of a lifetime of institutional care.

But the Axelles, deeply religious, appealed the verdict to their God and chose to fight it. They took Dack home, and Patty, his mother, gave up her career in nursing to be with him. By sheer force of will, she taught him to stand and even take a few steps with a walker. "He'd scream," she says, "but I just kept doing it." She got him walking with crutches and braces; his dad took him swimming at the Y.

And then Dack decided, at the age of eight, on a larger challenge: entering the 5-mile division of the Richmond marathon. "It's not whether you finish first or last, it's that you finish," Dave, Sr., told him. Dack did. The next year he moved up to 13 miles and finished that, too.

When he was ten, he wanted to try the whole 26.2- mile course. His mother was against it, but Dack kept on training secretly with his dad to go the distance. When the day came, he wasn't so sure he could. At 20 miles, he was thinking about quitting until he passed a lawn party and heard a stereo playing the theme from "Rocky" just for him. He kept going. At 23 miles, he and his father stopped to pray, and Dave, Sr., suggested dropping out.

"I want to go a little further," said Dack.

He did, on raw desire, heaving his body along on his crutches for the last three miles. The race took him 11½ hours and he was among the last to finish. But when he turned the corner of Twelfth and Main into the final block, the crowd was cheering Dack as if he had won. He had won — the test of his own character.

Dack is twenty years old now, in his junior year of college and majoring in political science. He has lost the use of his legs, but still competes in wheelchair marathons throughout the state, winning the opportunity to participate in the first wheelchair marathon staged in Russia in 1991. Dack credits the support of a loving family for his persistence and courage, and when asked if he has any advice to give others with disabilities to overcome, says simply, "*Never give up!*"

♦ ♦ ♦

Michael Magevney did what most typical college freshman would do over spring break: he partied on the beach, tanning, drinking, and playing in the sand. A friend talked him into trying something different the second time around.

Giving Others a Break

Nashville, Tennessee

Michael Magevney's first spring break "was exactly like you see on TV," he remembered. "There were young women doing bikini contests and kegs of beer everywhere. I thought that was what spring break was supposed to be like, but I came back exhausted, sunburned, and more tired than when I left."

One year later, on the advice of a friend, Magevney was scraping, sanding, and painting the house of a ninety-year-old Nashville resident, sleeping on the floor of the local YMCA at night.

94

A Vanderbilt sophomore at the time, Magevney gave up his vacation to do volunteer service. "By staying in Nashville it almost made the experience more powerful because I didn't have to leave my own backyard. The woman's house was only four or five miles from campus, but it was night and day from what I had ever seen."

As interest in social activism has increased among twentysomethings, the demand for "alternative" spring breaks — where students spend their vacation time volunteering in communities — has skyrocketed. This year, more than twelve thousand students will participate in service-oriented spring break programs coordinated by national groups such as Break Away and Habitat for Humanity International. Countless others will take part in breaks organized by their local colleges.

"Students want to do something new, different, and challenging in their free time," says Magevney, who, after his powerful experience, went on to found the alternative break program, Break Away. "A lot of students don't really want to just go home or go party over their vacations. People want to do different things, and this is where alternative breaks have found their niche."

With the help of fellow Vanderbilt undergraduate Laura Mann, Magevney founded Break Away in 1991 to facilitate alternative spring breaks for college students around the country. The program provides advice to students and nonprofits on how to start and run alternative breaks. It also matches college groups with local organizations that need volunteer help. While participation varies among schools, colleges often send small groups ranging in size from ten to twenty people to a number of different locations where community service work is needed.

Today more than three hundred member schools pay a nominal fee to use the Break Away SiteBank. This continuously updated database provides a comprehensive list of potential work sites for an alternative break program. Subscribers are put in touch with community leaders as well as other schools that have gone to the same location in previous years.

"Break Away seeks to provide a stimulating and unforgettable experience," says Magevney. The organizers hope to leave participants more committed to a life of social action. "We don't want students to just go into a community without learning about the social, political, and economic issues it faces," he says.

Participants stress that learning about different communities, cultures, and environments is one of the highlights. "I had never been on a program where you go and live in a different community and participate in service," says Vicki, a sophomore at the University of Miami who spent last year's break reconstructing flood-damaged houses in Illinois. "Working with the people was definitely the best part," she says.

Other large nonprofits like Habitat for Humanity — which former President Jimmy Carter has been involved in for many years, and which works with low-income people throughout the world to build decent, affordable houses — have recently begun to coordinate spring breaks as well. Habitat's Collegiate Challenge program, started in 1987, anticipates having forty-five hundred students from over two hundred schools working at over a hundred sites building homes for low-income families.

Habitat for Humanity has more than a

hundred collegiate affiliates nationwide and holds fast to its ecumenical Christian foundation. " 'Theology of the Hammer' is a part of our Christian Heritage," says Lisa Osankan, who coordinates projects at Habitat. "We can set everything else aside as long as you can work side by side with people building houses for people in need."

Start-up programs may run into problems coordinating breaks with communities thousands of miles away. By training student leaders and helping to coordinate breaks, groups like Break Away and Habitat for Humanity hope to save schools from making mistakes that can damage relations between a school and a community.

Some colleges manage just fine by coordinating volunteer breaks on their own. Georgetown University in Washington, D.C., for example, has one of the oldest break programs in the United States. The school, which has been sending students to the Appalachian region for twenty years, sends ninety students to six different sites in the mountainous area in an average year.

"One of the main purposes of these breaks is to heighten awareness among college students," said Sean Burns, a Georgetown senior and organizer of the school's break program. "If you can get people aware as early as possible of what's going down in other places, it may help in the long run."

Or, as Linda Chisholm, president of the Association of Episcopal Colleges, says, "To be in class and constantly thinking about social problems but not having any way of addressing them is a very discouraging and disheartening thing. To be a participant and know that you are trying to make things better for a community is an important part of finding out who you are and what your place is."

For more information on Break Away, or other programs, call (615) 343-0385.

CHAPTER 4

THE OLD AND THE BOLD — OUR CLASSIC CITIZENS

When grace is joined with wrinkles, it is adorable. There is an unspeakable dawn in a happy old age.

—Victor Hugo

Interview with Art Linkletter

A Happy Old Age. To millions of Americans, this ideal state is a reality. How they are doing it is a lesson for everyone fortunate enough to follow in their footsteps. The late Maggie Kuhn, founder of the Gray Panthers, said, "old age is not a disease — it's a triumph. Because you've survived. Failure, sickness, loss — you're still here." The stories in this chapter are outstanding examples of ordinary folks who have chosen to make the best of the rest of their lives, and their actions dispel the most common myth about old age — the one about rocking chairs.

But many negative perceptions about the elderly persist, and most of them are myths that need to be corrected. To get an update on the state of this "Old and Bold" generation, I asked one of their leading advocates, who is eighty-three himself, for an interview. He is Art Linkletter, a fixture for over sixty-two years on radio and TV — in *House Party* and *People Are Funny*, and author of twenty-three books, including *Old Age Is Not for Sissies*.

Art Linkletter is not retired. Far from it. Today, he lectures nationwide on a variety of inspirational subjects and, in addition to his many business interests, serves as vice-chairman of the Center for Aging at the University of California, Los Angeles, and is chairman of the board of directors of the John Douglas French Alzheimer Research Foundation, a worldwide center for research and development of a cure for Alzheimer's disease.

According to Mr. Linkletter, many of the stereotypes about the elderly came about naturally, because before 1940 there was no such thing as geriatric care, or even pediatric care, and the result was that doctors gave the same prescriptions and looked at diseases the same way whether you were two or ninety. Linkletter says, "Now all that's been replaced by highly specialized understanding of the nature of human growth and aging. When I wrote my book, *Old Age Is Not for Sissies*, I ran into a lot of the myths. I did the research for the book largely through focus groups of people that I sat around with and talked with all over the country with long-playing tapes and let them correct certain thoughts people have about aging."

Mr. Linkletter confirmed the following census figures for growth of the elderly over the next forty years:

- The population of people over sixty-five will double.
- The population of people over eighty-five will triple.
- The population of people over one hundred will grow the fastest, with over 1.4 million people in this age group by 2035.

When I asked Art Linkletter what he considered to be the secret of a happy old age, he replied, "The great secret of a happy old age is to have something to do that pleases you . . . which, by the way, is the secret of all life since you were born." And the greatest gift of old age? "Wisdom," Art said without hesitation. "Wisdom is reserved for the old. You can't get it while you are young. Everyone over sixty-five should receive an Honorary Doctorate of Life." Art Linkletter couldn't conclude the interview without adding some of his trademark humor. "One of the other great gifts of old age is — we can now become friends with our children."

—Interview with Art Linkletter printed with permission of the TV and radio star, author, businessman.

♦ ♦ ♦

He had kept the dream alive for sixty-six years, and now Norman Vaughan was going to fulfill it on . . .

The Peak of His Life

Trapper Creek, Alaska

The young man who went to Antarctica in 1928 with Admiral Richard E. Byrd is now old.

With his lined face, thin white hair, age spots and white beard, Norman Vaughan looks all of his now 89 years. But on Dec. 16, 1994, when most of us were planning holiday assaults on shopping malls, Norman Vaughan was on a glistening white mountaintop in Antarctica, 3,000 feet above the polar plain, 10,302 feet above sea level, 243 miles from the South Pole.

"It was quite a small top," he says. "It was breakable crust. We looked to the north and could see Vaughan Glacier that sloped to Scott Glacier. At one time, I looked out and counted 85 peaks. Only 2 to 3 percent of them have been climbed." Three days short of his 89th birthday — and after a nine-day, straight-up trek from the base camp — he became the first human to set foot on the summit of Mount Vaughan in the Queen Maud Range of the southernmost continent. When Admiral Byrd said, 'I've named a mountain after you,' I said . . . "I want to climb it,' " Vaughan said while visiting the National Geographic Society headquarters in Washington, D.C. The story of the climb was told in a "National Geographic Explorer" episode that aired on April 2, 1995, on the TBS cable channel.

It took Vaughan 66 years to realize his dream. He was a student at Harvard when he read the headline "BYRD TO THE SOUTH POLE" in a Boston newspaper. The journey sounded better than studies, so Vaughan turned up without an appointment at the Boston home of Byrd, then a Navy commander, who was about to take the first expedition of U.S. explorers deep into Antarctica.

He ended up going south with Byrd's 1928–30 expedition. Vaughan was the first U.S. citizen to drive dogs in Antarctica, and he became Byrd's chief dog driver. His college friends Edward Goodale and Freddy Crockett also drove dogs during the expedition. Byrd named a mountain after each of the three. Vaughan never returned to his classes. He went on to drive dogs for a medical mission in Newfoundland and in World War II, when he served in the Army Air Forces with 425 dogs under his command. His dogs, sled and drivers rescued wounded soldiers during the Battle of the Bulge. He raced dogs in the 1932 Olympics, the only time dog racing has been part of the Games.

Sled dogs are still a part of his life. Vaughan and his wife, 51-year-old Carolyn Muegge-Vaughan, keep as many as 40 dogs at their one-room log cabin at Trapper Creek in the Alaska outback, more than three hours from Anchorage.

"Good Alaskan mongrels," Muegge-Vaughan says. Both have run dog teams in Alaska's tough Iditarod race.

On December 16, 1994, Carolyn Muegge-Vaughan was right behind her husband on Mount Vaughan in the 24-hour Antarctic summer daylight. "Just before I got to the top, I shouted, 'Carolyn! Only two more steps!'" Vaughan says.

Three weeks after reaching the summit, the triumph in his voice was still unmistakable as he was being interviewed. And understandable. Not only did he wait six decades for the moment, but this particular expedition was delayed a year when the supply plane for their 1993 expedition crashed in Antarctica.

No one was hurt, but the crash was a blow. The airplane remains where it came down, with much expensive equipment still aboard. Of the 20 dogs on board, four — Sticker, Magoo, Pudge and Pandy — were lost when they wandered away after the crash.

The 1994 expedition flew in to the base camp at Mount Vaughan. There were no dogs this time, a disappointment for the Vaughans. An international treaty banning non-native animals and plants from the continent took effect after the failed 1993 effort. Instead, the Vaughans, with Alaska climber and guide Vern Tejas, and a National Geographic film crew, took eight days to climb the two horizontal miles and 3,000 vertical feet of the mountain.

Temperatures in the Antarctic summer range from 20 degrees below zero to 10 degrees above, with winds as high as 60 mph. Because the bones are fused in one of Vaughan's ankles and one of his knees is artificial, he couldn't zigzag sideways up the mountain but had to attack the slope head-on. With his ice ax and boots, Tejas cut more than 7,000 steps in the crusty snow for Vaughan, usually working about 30 feet ahead.

"It's a treat to climb with Norman," Tejas says. "We needed to pace things back a bit. Norman has a very strong spirit, but he does have the body of an 89 year-old. An 89 year-old body is much slower."

Vaughan is going on the lecture circuit now, talking about the importance of dreams. "I want people to dream big," he says. "I think that young people and older people should have dreams. People should look forward to retirement but should not think of it in terms of an armchair."

—By Hollis L. Engley
 Courtesy Gannett News Service.

◆ ◆ ◆

Three distinguished gentlemen, all retired, and having a good time at it, were sitting around one day eating ice cream. Out of the blue, they decided to form a group to help the people less fortunate than themselves . . . they called it:

The Old Fogies

Charlotte, North Carolina

In 1992, Joe Snyder and his pals decided they should do more than eat ice cream. They formed The Old Fogies, a volunteer group that cooks and delivers hot meals to Charlotte's Emergency Winter Shelter.

Once a month, they divide themselves into groups of casserole makers and bread-and-butter spreaders and whip up enough food for 190 men to have a meal and a second helping.

"It's a fun social thing," says Snyder. "There's a camaraderie that's developed among ourselves. But mainly, you feel you're doing some good for somebody."

The Fogies are part of the changing face of volunteers. More and more, nonprofit groups are relying on "nontraditional" helpers — such as senior citizens, teenagers, college students, and workers who persuade employers to let them take time off during the day to help out.

"We have a lot of elderly folks that help us," says Jim Gabriels, director of the Emergency Winter Shelter. "It's helpful when anybody comes in and lends a hand."

The Old Fogies, who live in the same area of Charlotte, had different reasons for pitching in. Some knew the importance of volunteer work. Others wanted to get involved.

For M. J. Boyd, seventy-nine, who grew up in Oklahoma during the Depression, it was personal. "My mother got sick when I was fifteen, and when I came out of high school, there were no jobs. My brother and I had to leave there and find work," he recalls.

"I thumbed it all over the country. Then I rode some freight trains looking for work. I put in applications — enough applications to paper a house. But everybody was looking for jobs then. . . . Finally, in 1940, I enlisted . . .

"I knew what it was like going without meals," he says. "I always said I postponed them, and would catch up with them later."

It's a cold Monday morning and The Old Fogies are relaxing in easy chairs, each with a cup of coffee in hand. They're in the living room of Joe Snyder's home. They're supposed to describe their work, but my, how they digress.

Mention that Ed Stephenson used to work for a cigar company and the discussion turns to the bestselling cigar. And recalling Jim Fosbrink's hole-in-one around his seventieth birthday prompts a discourse on golf.

Their backgrounds are varied, but they share many interests, including retirement. Burl Burnham, at eighty-four, is the oldest. "You're not eighty-four, Burl," Jim Fosbrink says. "Well, I'm eighty-three. I'll be eighty-four in a few months."

"And here I thought Boyd was the oldest," Fosbrink says. "I've been giving all my fatherly respect to Boyd." The men crack up.

Snyder, the second youngest at sixty-two, tells how The Old Fogies began. "Most of the wives in the neighborhood belong to a garden club," he says in a deep, commanding voice. "When they would get together, the men would go out for a hot fudge sundae.

"After a while, we decided we should do more than eat ice cream, although we still do a lot of that. I had worked with the homeless shelter for a year, so I asked around to see if anybody would want to start cooking meals for the men. Everyone accepted."

Jim Fosbrink cuts in.

"Joe has been the common thread for this group," says Fosbrink, a white-haired, smiling man who enjoys a good joke. "We all knew Joe, but we didn't know each other. We call him our fearless leader."

Frank Cann, who bears an uncanny resemblance to former Surgeon General C. Everett Koop, adds: "Our letterhead used to list 'Chief Fogy' and 'Associate Fogies,' but we've toned it down." "Here is our lineup . . ."

Snyder, who's retired from the Navy, organized the group with military precision. They prepare a meal for each of the four months of the year the Emergency Winter Shelter is open.

Instead of serving cold sandwiches in paper bags, The Old Fogies fix hot meals. "It's not that much more expensive," Snyder says. "It's a little more work, but the work is half the fun."

The week before they're scheduled to do a meal, Snyder distributes the marching orders. "To: The Old Fogies," his memo reads.

Names, phone numbers, and the menu are listed. Teams are set up. Work assignments distributed. Car pools arranged. The shopping list handed out. They devote an afternoon to shopping.

"That's a whole 'nother outing," says Bob McCoy, over on the sofa next to

Snyder. "We go around to where we get the best prices, and it usually takes more than three hours, depending on whether we eat ice cream or not."

The following day, they divide into cooking teams. Then they set out for the shelter, on West Fourth Street, loaded down with Crock-Pots of spaghetti sauce and steamer trays filled with macaroni and cheese.

The Old Fogies provide extras too: they pass out pieces of candy. They leave magazines. They put cinnamon in their applesauce!

"When they come through the line, we ask them, 'Did you get enough of this?' or 'Be sure you try some of that,' " says Burl Burnham. "For them to feel that somebody respects them means a lot."

Snyder and a few other Old Fogies return at five the next morning to serve coffee. The Old Fogies say they've learned a lot. "I know how to make macaroni and cheese," Jim Fosbrink says. The men laugh, then get serious.

Frank Cann says quietly: "I used to dodge the homeless or look away. Now I feel more compassion for them."

Says M. J. Boyd: "We don't know what it is until we walk in those guys' shoes.

We never know the circumstances that put them there."

And L. C. Perry, a former Charlotte police officer, agrees. "I always think [of the verse] 'There but for the grace of God go I.' "

◆ ◆ ◆

Don't talk about mandatory retirement plans to Fred Hartnett of Florida. Besides still being active as a real estate broker . . .

At 93, Legal Guardian
Has No Plans to Retire

Coral Gables, Florida

Fred Hartnett is no stranger to hard work. A former commissioner and mayor of Coral Gables in the late 1940's and 1950's, he owned a real estate and insurance agency and still is active as a broker at Hartnett Realty.

Hartnett, who turns 94 in 1995, also goes to work every day at the law office of John M. Thomson, where he acts as a personal representative and legal guardian for the elderly.

In 1994, Hartnett was the oldest finalist for the Florida You're Still Ticking award, sponsored by Timex. The award, presented by the Florida Department of Elder Affairs and Labor and Employment Security, calls attention to the value of older workers and encourages private industry to employ more of the elderly.

"He's an outstanding senior citizen," said Thomson, who nominated Hartnett for the award. "To have a 93-year-old man to take care of 'youngsters' in their 80's is a real plus. They bond with him," Thomson said. "The courts like it and he does all the leg work."

Hartnett was appointed by the probate court to be the personal representative for the estates of two elderly people who had died without wills. He settled the estates to the satisfaction of the many heirs, said Thomson, who deals with elder law.

He was also appointed by the court to serve as the legal guardian of another couple, ages 88 and 90, who live in a nursing home. He visits them regularly and takes care of their needs. He also looks over papers, signs the checks and pays the bills.

Hartnett likes keeping busy. "It keeps

my mind off of any little ills or quirks I might have," he said.

Fred arrived in Coral Gables from Fulton, N.Y., in 1925. He and his first wife, Elizabeth, who died in 1975, had five sons. He has 16 grandchildren and 15 great-grandchildren.

Hartnett has been a volunteer for the Catholic Church and the St. Vincent De Paul Society for 68 years.

Wife Marge, whom he married in 1976, says he gets up every morning about 6:30, has breakfast, attends Mass, and goes to work five days a week.

Hartnett has no plans to retire.

"Maybe some day when I get old enough," he said. "Right now I have no alternate plans."

—By Bea Moss
Times Herald, August 25, 1994.
Reprinted with permission of
Knight-Ridder Tribune News
Service.

◆ ◆ ◆

Stanley Galczynski doesn't have to remember the good old days when neighbors all knew each other and looked out for one another, because he does that today, as . . .

Bloomfield Street's Good Neighbor

Dorchester, Massachusetts

There are many stories circulating on Dorchester's Bloomfield Street about Stanley Galczynski — how he drove Dorothy Terry to buy windows for her drafty home and fixed Sylvia Pittman's front fence. On Thanksgiving he brought a turkey to a single mother a few doors down, at Christmas it was a Polish ham.

But the kindnesses Galczynski, 72, performs for free go further than fixing a gutter or a meal. Neighbors say he's helped recapture a feeling on Bloomfield Street some of Boston's streets have lost: a sense of community.

"I grew up in Roxbury and Dorchester and back then you knew your next-door neighbor, you looked out for each other," says Pittman, 40, who lives next door to Galczynski in the Fields Corner section. "Now it doesn't happen as much in some places, but it happens here. We look out for each other. He's helped that."

At a time when social service workers say some of the city's elderly are so frightened of crime they hesitate to befriend people, Galczynski and his wife, Marianna, 71, stand out as an inspiration to others to become more involved.

While community activities cite dozens of residents like the Galczynskis who make a difference, they say few are as old and as active.

"A lot of elderly people don't feel as safe as they used to," says Deahdra Butler-Henderson, director of Citizens for Safety, an anti-crime group. "But it helps to realize there are pockets in every community where [the] elderly feel so connected they feel safe. It helps the neighborhood, people watch out for each other."

Galczynski, a Polish immigrant who suffered through a five-year ordeal in the Nazis' Buchenwald concentration camp, has lived on Bloomfield Street for 22 years with his wife. His three children are grown and two live out of state. He has no other relatives in the U.S.

Bloomfield Street's residents have changed in those years, Galczynski says, from predominately white to a diverse mixture of African-Americans, Hispanics and Asians. He doesn't keep track of the names of all the people who have moved in over the years on the 51-home road between Greenbriar Street and Geneva Avenue.

"But I know them by their faces," Galczynski says, who starts down the street around 6 A.M. every morning to buy his paper around the corner. He walks up and down the street and throughout the neighborhood several times a day, for exercise and to pay social calls.

"I watch out for my neighbors, all of them. I feel good when I do things. I know what it means to help each other out," he says. "We are all friends here."

Bloomfield Street had some crime that made the newspapers about eight years ago — a murder and drug problems, according to newspaper stories and residents. The street has less crime now, community officials and police say.

"We very rarely go to Bloomfield Street now and it's because of the people who live there," said Boston police Sgt. Tom Flanagan, who works in community services.

"I like people who live on my street," says Galczynski, who worked in Santa Maria Hospital's housekeeping department in Cambridge for 37 years before retiring in 1988. "I bring encyclopedias to a neighbor. They are maybe old, but they are good and the neighbors are happy. They help me too, they shovel my walk."

In the summer, Galczynski sits on his wide porch with Marianna and watches the street. In the winter, they call on neighbors they haven't seen in a while to make sure they are OK.

"He is the eyes and ears of this street and is the ideal neighbor," says Barbara Trybe who lives near Galczynski. Trybe works for Healthy Boston, a city-run social service neighborhoods program. "Some elderly people in the city are afraid to go out, but he helps everyone."

—By Beth Daley
The Boston Globe, February 3, 1995.
Reprinted with permission of
Knight-Ridder Tribune News
Service.

◆ ◆ ◆

Sitting on the sidelines of a track and field meet, watching her son Wendell compete in the fifty-five-meter dash and throw the shot put, Margaret White was just like any proud mother — cheering her son along. The only difference was that her son Wendell was sixty-two, and she was ninety-eight. "Hey Mom, why don't you get out here too?" became a rallying cry for this feisty lady.

The Hundred-Year-Old Shot-Putter from Turpin, Oklahoma

Turpin, Oklahoma

Margaret White worked for fifty cents an hour during the Depression, raised ten children by herself, and outlived two husbands.

In 1995, at the age of one hundred, she was one of 142 amateur athletes who competed in the track and field events in Oklahoma City at the Sooner State Games; a part of the U.S.A. Track and Field Masters program. Her event is the shot put. She easily won the competition for her age group in January with a throw of eleven feet two inches. Her career best throw was twelve feet eleven inches, "But she was just ninety-eight back then," said her son, Wendell Palmer, sixty-two, of Pampa, Texas. "And plus, we only had a four-kilogram shot. We didn't have a three-kilo one at the time."

"Old people like me ought to do *something* to stay active," Mrs. White said in a telephone interview from her home in the Oklahoma panhandle town of Turpin, where she lives alone, except for occasional visits from her children.

Here's how Margaret stays active: She takes a six-pound ball of iron, presses it against her chin, crouches, spins, and thrusts it as far as she can.

White moved to Turpin three years ago from Liberal, Kansas, to be closer to her children. Son Wendell had become involved in senior Olympic-type events, running the fifty-five-meter dash and throwing the shot.

One day, he jokingly asked his mother, "Why don't you come out with us?"

She said, "Well, I might just do that." "We set her up at a meet in Pampa and she's been going every year," Wendell said. "She has her ups and downs, but she really gets high when we get to talking about going to a meet. She's got a pretty strong will."

When the weather is warm, White takes her shot outside to practice. Her technique, not likely to be seen in instruction videos, is surprisingly sound.

"She tries to do it as close to legal as

possible," said Wendell. "There's no fancy glide at the end. She just steps through it and hooks it out there."

White said all of her children were active in sports, but she never had time for sports herself. Her first husband died when the ten children were young, and she spent all her time working and raising them.

She remarried in 1954; her second husband died in 1977. "I've had pretty good health, but I'm getting to be pretty well used up," she said. "I don't see too good. I don't always hear too good, but I still get around. I think I've done good for my age."

The Sooner State Games organizers were thrilled to have her compete. "I think it's fantastic," spokesman Robbie Robertson said. "The games promote mass participation. Last year we had a four-year-old figure skater, and this year, with Mrs. White, we have a hundred-year-old shot-putter."

Margaret White is taking all this attention in stride, even though the news of her senior shot put efforts has spread nationwide, including an appearance on *The Tonight Show* with Jay Leno.

She seems more concerned about her

son Wendell, who also still competes in the games. "Wendell is getting of an age that I don't think he ought to do it much longer," she said. Spoken like a true mother.

◆ ◆ ◆

This is a love story so moving, so powerful, it made the front page of The Wall Street Journal. *And maybe that makes sense. If the institution of marriage had a stock offering, you would want to invest in Joseph and Eva Solymosi's.*

After Seven Decades, Couple Still Finds Romance in the 90s

Florida

"Well, I tell you," says Eva Solymosi, and so she does, starting at the beginning when she first met Joseph. The youngest of 13, she was a poor cook in Hungary, befriended by an old woman who shared this advice: "When a kind face comes by, keep him."

Eva saw Joseph, an 18-year-old chimney sweep, getting a drink of cold water by the public well. "He had a kind face. So that's it," she says and shrugs. They

124

married the next year, moved to the U.S., and have been together since. She is 97 and he is 93. They live in a pink house because as a young girl, Eva dreamed of one; it is in Florida, because that was Joseph's dream.

Last fall, Mr. and Mrs. Solymosi celebrated their 75th wedding anniversary. They went to Mass where a priest gave Eva flowers, her husband an extra sprinkle of holy water and said, experienced as they were, they need not renew marriage vows. Mr. Solymosi bought a new dark suit. His wife got her first clothes dryer. She is still not used to it, having spent a lifetime hanging clothes on the line.

"To me, I live the old way," Eva says, her accent and idioms thick with the Old World. "I don't go for new things." The dryer is nice, but the clothes get too dry, she says, making them difficult to fold neatly. You wouldn't know. Joseph opens the linen closet, where stacks of sheets sit ironed, folded and held together by a pink satin ribbon. "That is all her work," he says with pride.

The couple never had any children. Although Joseph wanted to adopt, Eva wanted "My own flesh and blood or none at all." Eva has a few nieces, but otherwise they have outlived their family and most of their friends. The Solymosis are in remarkably good health, even though she says her eyesight is failing and every once in a while, she catches her mind napping. "I'm going to be 100 years old. That has to take something from the body," she says. She doesn't bother with a calendar. Each day is enough.

Roses and Roadsters

Joseph has arthritis, and gave up cutting the lawn last year. His mind is clear: He remembers their lot on 105th Street in Cleveland measured 31-by-117 feet, just enough for Eva's 100 tulips and 30 rosebushes, although he is less sure whether he once paid $87 or $89 for a Ford Roadster. A former chauffeur, he has had six cars, one accident in the 1930's, and three flat tires. He has never run out of gas and his license, recently renewed, doesn't expire until 1999. He loves to drive but limits excursions to the grocery store, the doctor's office and church for 4 P.M. Mass Saturday — his 1972 Buick Le Sabre has 51,109 miles on it. For him, driving on roads under construction is a thrill. "You go this way and that way. Boy, you just get a darned big kick out of it," he says.

Eva's passion is a clean house, which is why she won't let her husband cook duck or geese. The fat splatters all over the stove, and one thing that gets her gander is a dirty stove. "Not even steel wool cleans it." Nor will she allow him to park in the garage after driving in the rain because the car drips on the clean floor. "I'm a fuss button," she says, without apology. Joseph doesn't mind. After 75 years, some things don't matter. "The older you get the closer you are," he said. "We must care for one another. I want to last for another 50 years."

The couple offers no great secrets to longevity and love. They married for better or worse. They were immigrants with little schooling, who worked hard and lived simply by her father's golden rules: "Always give people a day's work for their dollar. Be honest. Be good and people will love you for it."

But it wasn't easy. Their first home in America was the second floor of a chicken coop at Bessie Miller's roadside restaurant in Cleveland, where they worked for $50 a month serving fried chicken dinners. When they celebrated their first Christmas in a two-room apartment, putting a tree at the foot of their bed, a visitor chided them, saying they were childish. "But we are children," Eva remembers telling her. "We never had a Christmas tree."

They spent most of their lives working for the Oscar Grody family in Cleveland. Hazel Grody, nine years old when they arrived, was the daughter they never had. Pictures of Hazel shoveling snow and feeding a squirrel, getting married, holding her babies and smiling with grandchildren fill their photo albums and bureau tops. "They were my family," says Eva, who kept their house clean. "We were poor. They didn't treat us like that. That meant more than anything to me."

Forever Young

The couple cared for Hazel's parents until they both died in 1965, sometimes spending the night when they were infirm. After the funeral, Eva cleaned the house, wrapping every linen and memento in heavy white paper, and labeling them as best she could phonetically.

Only then would they agree to retire and move to Florida.

"They were faithful to the end," says Hazel Grody Rosensteel. "And they are to this day. In their eyes, I can do no wrong. I'm still nine years old." Now 77, she calls them at least once a week, and periodically makes the four-hour drive to visit them, her own health permitting. She has known them longer than she knew her own parents, who have been gone nearly 30 years. She was two years old when Joseph and Eva married.

Actually, Joseph says, it was Eva who married him. Eva laughs, "Yes, I was the wrecker. I wrecked your life." They tease each other gently. When she moves ahead of him in a story, he scolds her, "Keep your shirt on, Charlie." He sometimes calls her "my friend" or "boss," although, he adds, neither one of them is the boss.

They are partners. When one is telling a story, the other quietly gets up and fetches a pertinent picture or letter. They share the chores and praise the other's efforts. Eva, who has her own pink tile bathroom, says she never has to clean Joseph's. "It's immaculate," she says.

Joseph does the grocery shopping, buying two of everything — coffee, vinegar, cereal. "Who knows tomorrow whether I can make the trip," he says. He is the more worldly one. He taught her to use the dryer and calmly explains when she laments about cheap furniture. "Eva, this is a fast world. It isn't anymore the slow world we had."

Storing Memories

They have been blessed, they say, not only with each other but with good friends. Look, they say. There's the dining room table from Hazel's grandmother, and the perfume from a lawyer and his wife who, before they died years ago, drove 70 miles to visit them every Sunday. Eva doesn't wear perfume but keeps the tiny bottles in a circle on her dresser. "I am a keeper," she says. "These things are precious because of the people." A five-year-old silk corsage from her 70th wedding anniversary rests in a plastic box in her drawer.

When Joseph is shopping or watching the news, Eva will spend hours going through her dozen photo albums. There is Joseph as a young man reading the newspaper, Eva eating an ear of corn in the 1920's, their first Christmas tree. Each album is like an old friend, inviting her back to her rose garden or to visit her mother's gravesite in Cleveland.

"I open it up and it gives me joy. To me it's something. To anyone else it means nothing," says Eva, almost apologetically. Joseph reassures her. "Oh Eva, it's wonderful. It's beautiful to look back."

She comes across a picture of him when he was 18. "Ah ha, that is the kind face I fell in love with. In my eyes he is still as handsome." He says nothing, but gently taps her cane with his.

—By Clare Ansberry

◆ ◆ ◆

Maybe it's because she was born in Hawaii; maybe it's because Daniel Boone was one of her ancestors, or maybe it's because she spent twenty-five years as a nurse tending people confined to hospital beds, but one thing's for sure

— Elizabeth Terwilliger just can't stand the indoors!

Mrs. T Leads the Way
Mill Valley, California

The outdoors is in Elizabeth Terwilliger's blood. She counts Kit Carson and Daniel Boone among her ancestors, and she has spent the past thirty-eight of her eighty-five years in active rebellion against the indoor society. As the head, heart, and soul of the Terwilliger Nature Education Center in Marin County, California, across the Golden Gate Bridge from San Francisco, she is a crusader for preserving open spaces — for bicycle paths, nature trails, wildlife sanctuaries, and butterfly preserves — and is especially passionate about getting children outside.

Seven days a week, almost 365 days a year, she leads groups of twenty-five to thirty-five school kids on guided tours of a world beyond their living rooms, teaching them to love the outdoors, she says, "because we take care of what we love." The thousands of kids she guides each year are from an indoor society that doesn't know a beaver from a muskrat. So Mrs. T, as everyone calls her, begins her field trips by introducing them to a menagerie of stuffed birds and beasts in her van. "Hello, Great White Egret! Hello, Mr. Turkey Vulture!" Then off they go to see the real thing.

Mrs. T is still a spry figure, leading the way in a straw hat, plaid shirt, and jeans, and her excitement is irresistible. "Knowledge dispels fear," she says, "and love comes in."

Several years ago at a White House award ceremony for volunteers, she seized her moment on stage to introduce yet another crowd of "indoorsmen" to the life outside. "*V* is for vulture," she exclaimed, her arms up in a *V* like a vulture's wings. President Reagan was standing behind her and, following Mrs. T's lead like thousands of kids before him, lifted his arms high and made a *V*, too.

CHAPTER 5

MAKING A DIFFERENCE: CARING, SHARING AMERICANS

Never doubt that a small group of thoughtful, committed citizens can change the world; indeed, it is the only thing that ever has.

—Margaret Mead

With the daily onslaught of news coverage devoted to death, drugs, and destruction; talk shows filled with screaming, dysfunctional people; and pessimistic sociologists and radical religious groups proclaiming the erosion or end of our country's moral values, is it any wonder most of us ask ourselves if there is any kindness or compassion left in the world?

Well, take heart, America. When Paul Newman was honored at the Academy Awards ceremony for his humanitarian work, he said, "In my estimation, the

United States is the most generous nation on the face of the planet." Mr. Newman knows his facts. Consider these statistics:

- Over ninety million Americans volunteer their time to help others each year.
- These volunteers donate an estimated twenty billion hours of free time each year.
- The value of this free time is estimated to be as high as $175 billion dollars.

That's wonderful, you say, but it must also be true that Americans are greedy, selfish individuals who spend their money only on themselves and their comforts while ignoring the needs of others. Wrong. In 1993, Americans gave *$126.2 billion* to charities of all kinds. Only 11.5 percent of that incredible sum came from foundations and corporations. The vast bulk — 88.5 percent — came from the pockets (or in some cases, the estates) of *individual* Americans.

The 1993 total was a new record. So was the 1992 total. And the one in 1990. In fact, the total amount of money given to charity in the United States has increased every year since 1959, which is when the Trust for Philanthropy, publishers of *The Chronicle of Philanthropy* (the authoritative source for these figures), began tracking charitable contributions.

Who are these caring givers, these sharing, compassionate people who give of their money, their time, their hearts, to make life a little better for others? They don't make the front pages for their kindness, nor do they seek such attention, but their unselfish humanitarianism needs to be given more prominence in order to remind us that far from being rare, such actions are the norm. As Goethe put it, "Kindness is the golden chain by which society is bound together."

Some of the stories in this chapter were found in the news media, but most were contributed by two organizations who are devoted to giving recognition to these outstanding, caring, sharing Americans. My thanks to the Positive Thinking Foundation, founded by the late Norman Vincent Peale and his wife Elizabeth Peale Allen. The foundation created and administers America's

Awards, also known as the "Nobel Prize of Goodness," which annually honors six unsung heroes who embody dedication, initiative, purpose, sacrifice, resourcefulness and tenacity. Thanks also go to The Caring Institute, and *Caring People Magazine* founded in 1985 by two brothers, Val and William Halamandaris, to "promote selflessness and public service." Each year the institute stages the National Caring Awards, honoring ten adults and ten young adults as the most caring people in America in order to "identify, honor, reinforce, and focus attention on caring."

The people chronicled in this chapter truly represent the asset side of our national balance sheet; their stories provide an insight into the kind of people we are and the kind of society we live in.

◆ ◆ ◆

Almost fifteen thousand dollars lay on the seat beside him, all in crisp ten-dollar bills. The unidentified driver steered his Cadillac into the Skid Row section of downtown L.A. An observer of this scenario might suspect all sorts of things —

a drug buy, a bookie collecting bets, but it's the Christmas season, and . . .

The Eldorado Elf Makes His Rounds

Los Angeles, California

Coasting through downtown L.A. aboard a Cadillac sleigh, the benefactor known only as the Eldorado Elf was handing out ten-dollar bills to the disheveled denizens of Skid Row this Christmas week. Some fifteen thousand dollars was handed out by the mystery Santa in what has been a twelve-year tradition at the Midnight Mission. The Eldorado Elf took over the duties after his colleague, known as the Cadillac Santa, died in 1992.

When Torrance car dealer Ronald Moran, eighty, died of pneumonia, the Midnight Mission thought it had seen the last of the wealthy St. Nick in the flashy car. But a friend decided to keep the holiday tradition alive.

"We're just elves carrying on the Cadillac Santa tradition. Yes, it's exhilarating and exciting," said the fifty-year-old benefactor, who identifies himself only as "Cadillac Santa's Elf."

Word spread quickly that a money-clutching man in a red 1994 Cadillac Eldorado was wheeling through Skid Row and heading toward the Midnight Mission.

"The ten-dollar man is here! The ten-dollar man is here!" were the cries echoing through the alleyways near Fourth and Los Angeles streets. Lines formed quickly and smiles bloomed over the usual faces of despair.

"They are lined up for blocks. There are smiles everywhere. It's really something," said mission director Clancy Imislund. "For once, they are getting something and nobody wants anything from them."

Richard Woods, fifty-four, a homeless man collecting his ten dollars said: "Wow! This made my day. Well, it's pretty nice, to tell you the truth."

The Eldorado Elf also passed on wisdom learned from the Cadillac Santa. "The Cadillac Santa said there were three stages of wealth," the benefactor said. "The first stage is when you make it. The second stage is fighting to keep it, and the third stage is when you give it all away.

"That is the most enjoyable stage of wealth."

◆ ◆ ◆

If you came to America as a young immigrant from Greece speaking no English, with less than thirty dollars in your pocket, and went on to achieve more success than you could ever imagine, how would you give thanks? A Pennsylvania restaurateur does it this way:

Uncle Lou's Picnic

Beaver County, Pennsylvania

In 1951, 20-year-old Elias Demetrious Papanikolaou, a.k.a. Louis Pappan, arrived at Ellis Island from his native Greece with two battered suitcases, a few dollars in his pockets and the address of an uncle in Beaver Falls, Pa.

Today, Lou Pappan owns 36 restaurants in Pennsylvania. He also has an obsession for sharing his good fortune.

He serves on many boards for non-profit organizations and has raised up to $400,000 a year for various causes, either through his restaurants or by personal buttonholing. Even after triple-bypass surgery three years ago, he is indefatigable.

During the Gulf War Pappan gave free

140

meals to the children of men and women serving in the desert. His restaurants provide menus in Braille for blind customers. He also sends a silver dollar to every baby born at The Medical Center in Beaver. And when the steel industry fell off sharply in western Pennsylvania in the 1980's and his business plummeted, Pappan refused to lay off a single employee.

But the event closest to the heart of "Uncle Lou," as he is known, is his annual "Uncle Lou's Picnic."

Held at Beaver County's Bradys Run Park, it is one of the world's largest, drawing more than 7,000 senior citizens from as far away as Kentucky and Virginia.

Besides mountains of food, there are free medical checkups for those who want one, entertainment, contests in needlework, baked goods, recipes, arts and crafts and ceramics, and prizes galore. Volunteers from his restaurants put in an 18-hour day preparing, serving and cleaning up, and insist it is the most rewarding workday of their year.

"Anyone can write a check. The important thing is to know why you're writing it," he says. "I'm only paying back what this country and its people did for me."

◆ ◆ ◆

In an ideal world, every school child gets a hot breakfast and a hug from mom and dad before leaving for school on those cold winter mornings. The reality is, many children receive nothing but the clothes on their back as they set out for school in the morning. It was like that for many kids in Roseville, California, until a group of volunteer women from the First Presbyterian Church began a program in which . . .

Kids Get Warm Hugs, Hot Food and Encouraging Words

Roseville, California

The sun crests the frosted rooftops, welcoming the first wave of steam-snorting kids lined up for a hot breakfast on their way to Roseville's Sierra Gardens Elementary School.

Only a few footsteps off the three-block

path between the low-income Pineridge Apartments and their school, the kids and a handful of mothers are there at 7:45 A.M. for scrambled eggs, blueberry muffins, fruit and milk. And for ketchup, used in great quantities by boys such as Scott Howard, 8, and his brother, Joseph Porter, 11, to decorate, disguise and disfigure the eggs.

Like so many doting mothers and grandmothers, 10 volunteers are there at the First Presbyterian Church to greet the pupils five days a week with hot food, warm hugs and encouraging words.

They have been at it 3½ years now; they say they will be there as long as they are needed.

The church women didn't have to look far for this worthy cause: These children traipsed by five days a week. Once they were angry, with the day's only hot meal still hours away at the midpoint of their school day. It ruined their appetite for learning and soured their attitude, said Dottie Poore, director of the Neighborhood Breakfast Program.

"We had some very angry children that first year," said Poore as she tallied attendance on a morning when more than 50 meals would be served. "Some of their parents were drug addicts, or doing time in jail. Some of the children were abused in more ways than one."

Poore has seen big changes in the way the kids look, act and feel.

"It has taken some time to settle them down, but this has turned into a safe haven for them," she said of the cabinsized building on a corner of the church property on Coloma Way. The cafeteria is a temporary one but there will be a permanent place for it within the planned two-story 55,000-square-foot family life center at the site. The First Presbyterian Church recently had its fellowship hall demolished to make room for the new building.

With volunteer labor and donated money, Poore and meal planner Dyann Moss are able to produce a daily hot breakfast meal for an average 62 cents.

Started with a memorial of $300 from a church member, the meal program subsists on about $400 a month. Roseville's elementary school district serves 3,000 hot lunches a day at a total of 12 sites but only one school, Woodbridge, offers breakfast. Because of district cafeteria limitations, it is a cold meal.

The Neighborhood Breakfast Program

has attracted diverse volunteers. Tami Forbes has three children and can't help in the morning, so she bakes 10 dozen muffins and delivers them for the Wednesday breakfast each week. This baking effort takes the better part of a day and consumes three 80-ounce boxes of muffin mix per week, she said.

On the receiving end are people like Ana Zacarias and her four children. The youthful mother's oldest is a boy in kindergarten at Sierra Gardens. She said the hot meal helps get her family started on school days.

"It helps with the budget too," she said.

Louise Isaacson, principal at Sierra Gardens, said the breakfast program has filled tummies and other empty spots in the children's lives.

"It's not only the warm food, it's the warm atmosphere that's provided there," she noted.

—By Jon Engellenner
Copyright, *The Sacramento Bee*, 1995,

♦ ♦ ♦

Alexander Graham Bell was an instructor to the deaf before he invented the telephone. He would be proud of the work of Louis Marracci and his colleagues in the Telephone Pioneers of America.

He Tinkers So Others Can Hear

LaFayette, California

There are several thousand deaf people who can hear and sightless people who can read because of the tireless efforts of Louis Marracci and his fellow volunteers in the Telephone Pioneers of America. The Pioneers is made up of 860,000 retired and active employees of U.S. and Canadian telephone companies and claims to be the largest industry-related volunteer organization in the world. It focuses on projects relating to education, the homeless, AIDS, and the environment.

Seventy-four-year-old Louis Marracci of Lafayette, California, puts in up to eighty hours a week as head of Project Fixit, a group of tinkerers who repair and refurbish hearing devices, teletype machines, and cassette players.

Marracci retired from Pacific Bell in 1977 after thirty-seven years with the company. His last job was district manager for construction in charge of laying and repairing cable in the San Francisco Bay area.

"I like the results," Marracci said of his avocation, "and if I didn't do this, I would vegetate. I can't sit all day and watch television."

Marracci is a former president of the Pioneers' George S. Ladd Chapter, which covers Marin, San Francisco, northern Alameda, and Contra Costa counties in California. He has been made "Pioneer activity coordinator and enabler," which puts him in charge of special projects.

Among the special projects was building a light-weight chair for a bicycle trailer so a disabled fourteen-year-old could take a cycling vacation with his family.

"That's when it gets emotional, when you can meet the person and see the result of your work," Marracci said.

Project Fixit began in 1991 when the Pioneers were given a stash of surplus, broken, and obsolete teletype devices used by the deaf to communicate across telephone lines. They refurbished them and donated them to police and sheriff's departments so they could communicate with deaf citizens.

Marracci and his merry band of repair-men didn't stop there. Working out of quarters at Pac Bell's central office in Oakland, California, they have churned out thousands of teletype machines, hearing aids, big-button telephones for the disabled, telephone amplifiers, and cassette players that are used to play back recorded books for the blind.

◆ ◆ ◆

For over thirty years, "Sweet Alice" Harris, as she is called, has tried to improve conditions for those who live among the pandemonium of drug and gang wars in the Watts district of Los Angeles. A recipient of the 1991 National Caring Awards, she is known as . . .

The Miracle Worker of Watts

Los Angeles, California

"Sweet" Alice Harris is a remarkable, tireless woman who has devoted her life to changing the lives of disadvantaged children and young adults in her often troubled community of Watts, in Los Angeles. She cares for every person who has ever asked for her help, without consideration of their color or circumstance.

Harris's work began out of her recognition of the needs of the Black and Hispanic communities. Harris observed fighting, stealing, and killing, often based on misunderstanding, both before and during the Watts riots.

"Both the Black and Hispanic communities wanted the same thing, but neither could speak the other's name. They both wanted better housing, education, jobs, and recreation for their children. They wanted the same thing; they just couldn't speak the language, so they would fight," Harris says. "But here now, black and brown sit together."

To ease the tensions in the community, years ago Harris began providing for some of the residents' common needs. If they needed a place to sleep, Harris found housing. If they needed food, Harris provided food. If they needed health care, Harris found health care. And if they needed education and a better life for their children, Harris provided it. "I never want to hear 'no' said, because it doesn't fit around here. I always want to be able to tell people they can eat, sleep, be counseled, and be comfortable, whenever we can serve their needs," explains Harris.

Harris, now in her sixties, was a teenage parent at age fourteen and was homeless when she was sixteen. "I understand what they are going through, and I understand that they expect to hear 'no,' because that's all they've ever heard. To wake up one day and have somebody say 'yes' to you, you really don't believe it. Finally, somebody helps you. Then, something just comes alive in you, and you put a smile on your face, and you want to live. The hope is alive, and when your hope is alive, you act and see differently. You can't do that saying 'no' to people. You just can't," says Harris, who never says "no" to anyone in need.

Over thirteen years ago, Harris formally founded Parents of Watts (POW) to encourage children to stay in school and stay off the drug-infested streets of their community. She now serves as the organization's executive director. Although POW has been incorporated since 1983, the program began informally in Harris's home thirty years ago with a group of volunteers addressing the basic needs of the poor in the Los

Angeles community. POW now offers over fifteen programs on a budget of $70,000, and the programs are run out of six properties that Harris has purchased.

Harris and her organization are involved in a variety of community issues. They provide emergency food and shelter assistance for the homeless every night. Approximately sixty-five single people are fed each night, and POW also gives out food to families. Over the holiday season, Harris and her volunteers delivered over two hundred additional food baskets to the area's poor and impoverished. In addition, twenty-three to thirty people sleep in the shelter every night.

A mobile medical team from the Watts Health Foundation also sees close to a hundred people every two weeks. Every child in the area now has had immunization shots, which was not the case before Harris's efforts.

POW also has a young mothers' program, which is designed to help young women become nurturing parents. It prepares unwed mothers to get their high school equivalency and to learn new job skills, as well as parenting skills. The center also provides counseling and drug abuse prevention. "Our private hospital has built a new wing for crack-dependent babies. That's a waste of money," comments Harris. "If they would help me catch them before they get to be crack-dependent, I could help. All I want is somebody to help me get to the drug-addicted women before they have their babies."

POW also sponsors amnesty for immigrants and offers classes to assist them to learn English. Harris also has played a key role in creating a harmonious relationship between the Hispanic, Korean, and Black communities during some very tense periods. It is no wonder that she is held in such high esteem by the community. In nominating Mrs. Harris for the National Caring Award in 1991, then Los Angeles Mayor Tom Bradley said, "While there are many Americans who could be identified for this recognition, I know of no person more deserving than Mrs. Harris, by virtue of the impact she has had in enriching and enhancing the lives of young people."

Although Harris serves the entire Watts community, it is the children and young adults with whom she has had the greatest impact. She promotes self-esteem and family stability as pivotal factors influencing the lives of children and young adults. Harris has provided numerous opportunities for high-risk youth who have no place to turn because their home environments are filled with drugs and violence.

In a week's time, Harris found on-the-job training for fifty young adults who would otherwise be loitering in the streets. Perhaps this is part of the reason she is often described as a "miracle worker" by her friends and colleagues.

"There is an old saying that you can lead a mule to the trough, but you can't make him drink. I'd like for people to say that Sweet Alice created a thirst, and the young people wanted to drink," explains Harris of her philosophy on youth and children.

Harris, who dropped out of school as a teen-ager and completed her bachelor of arts degree only in the last few years, knows the importance of a good education. For the entire community, classes in math, English as a second language, Spanish, reading improvement, Graduate Equivalency diploma (GED) preparation, computer skills, photography, auto mechanics and body repair, graphic arts, secretarial skills, upholstery, and woodworking/cabinet making are provided. Tutoring is also available. Over 110 potential high school dropouts, who were tutored at or attended classes at POW, have gone to college using resources from POW's community development department.

In 1986, POW sponsored a program that bused 40 teenagers from South Central Los Angles to attend Morristown College, a rural, Black junior college in Tennessee. Thirty-eight of the students earned associate of arts degree, and most went on to higher education. Harris was instrumental in gaining acceptance for these young adults into Morristown College and accompanied them on their bus trip. She firmly believed that the students needed to be away from drugs and the fast-paced city life so that they could concentrate on their studies.

"Sweet Alice cares for you regardless of your race or who you are, and all of the youth care for her in return. Anyone can call her at 3 A.M. for help, and she will be there — no matter where you are! Once, a young lady came to the center and said her mother was very ill in Mexico. Sweet Alice flew to Mexico just to offer words of encouragement to the woman. She never questions the need — she just gives," explains her assistant, Maudine Clark.

Mike Stewart, deputy to Council-woman Joan Miley Flores, echoed Clark's thoughts: "Alice Harris organized Parents of Watts to keep children off the streets and in the schools. She is responsible for better education in the Watts district. She has provided housing in a safe, clean environment for young adults in college, and has prepared unwed mothers to receive their GED and rear their babies properly. She has fought 'red-lining' in the city (an illegal practice whereby families of certain zip codes are not considered for loans, financing, or other services), for better roads, for improved housing, and for bringing rapid transit to the city in the form of a light rail or subway system to serve the inner-city residents. She's taught Spanish to Blacks and English to Hispanics and home ownership to the community."

Harris, who was selected as *Ms.* Magazine's 1988 Woman of the Year, helps those who would otherwise fall through the cracks of the welfare system. As Harris herself says, "The poor are going to be among us always, and they do need help. Everybody has got what the world needs. Whatever it is, even if it's just a smile, give it up. If you'll give back what God gave you, God will turn around and give it back to you again. It's like a flow of energy, the more you give, the more you receive. It's simple. The key to life is giving."

—By Sarah Anderson
Reprinted with permission of *Caring People Magazine*, Val J. Halamandaris, Publisher.

♦ ♦ ♦

She's one of the nation's most success-ful women. Her daily talk show has the highest ratings, without resorting to the weird and the abhorrent. Her company, Harpo Productions, is recognized as a producer of quality films and program-ming. A survivor of sexual abuse, she helped bring about the National Child Protection Act. A chance meeting with a teenage boy and his family in Chicago's poverty-stricken public housing led to what may well be Oprah Winfrey's greatest accomplishment.

Oprah Winfrey's Families for a Better Life

Chicago, Illinois

A mother living in a Chicago public housing development desperately wants to get off welfare, go back to school, and find a good job to help support her two daughters. Another family wants to move to a neighborhood where gangs, drugs, and violence aren't lurking on every street corner.

Both families are struggling against great odds to create a brighter future for their children. Both families want a chance to break free from the depressing cycle of welfare, poverty, and despair.

These scenarios reflect the harsh reality faced by many of the fifty thousand callers nationwide who responded to the Jane Addams Hull House Association of Chicago and Oprah Winfrey's announcement of a pilot program called Families for a Better Life. Oprah recently joined with Hull House Association to launch this comprehensive program aimed at helping low-income families move from subsidized housing to independent living.

"All the callers show there are real stories behind the statistics," says Gordon Johnson, Hull House Association president. "It puts a voice to the need and it also shatters the myth that all people who are on welfare or in public housing want to stay there."

Unlike other programs, Families for a Better Life takes an individualized and hands-on approach to meeting each family's needs by offering housing assistance, job training, health care, financial planning, family counseling, educational opportunities, and other long-term support services from Hull House Association.

Oprah has pledged six million dollars (three million of her own money and three million in matching funds to be raised by her) to launch this innovative and moving experiment in localized welfare reform. Families for a Better Life will eventually enroll one hundred Chicago families, each of whom will be moved from public housing, given the above support services from Hull House, and aided financially to the tune of thirty thousand dollars annually for an average of two years.

"No one makes it alone," Oprah says. "Everyone who has achieved any level of success in life was able to do so because something or someone served as a beacon to light the way. What seems to be an endless cycle of generational poverty and despair can be broken if each of us is willing to be a light to the other. When you learn, teach. When you get, give."

In 1994, while filming her television movie *There Are No Children Here* in a Chicago public housing development, Oprah met thirteen-year-old Kalvin, who lived in the Henry Horner housing project. "Kalvin," Oprah said, "marched up to me, said he was different from so many of the other kids he saw around him, and that he really wanted to succeed." Impressed, Oprah began seeing Kalvin often. She helped to tutor him, bought him school supplies, and listened as he talked of having been homeless and of now living with his mother and four siblings in a small apartment at Horner. The sound of gunfire, Kalvin said, was frequent; the quality of nearby schooling, abysmal.

Oprah decided to do something. She

decided, in fact, to take Kalvin to live with her in her luxurious lakefront apartment. "Whoa," said her fiancé, Stedman Graham. "You can't just take him away from his family. You have to help all of them." And so, Families for a Better Life was born.

Kalvin's family became the first in the pilot group, with nine other families being selected in February of 1995. These first ten families will be drug free, demonstrate a motivation and readiness to undergo change, and participate in an intense screening process, including an eight-week preparation training course. These sessions will help families make an informed decision and realistically assess what they can expect to encounter on their road to self-sufficiency and independent living.

Oprah, for her part, remains intimately involved with Families for a Better Life. She sees Kalvin frequently and talks with his mother Eva and the other children. "This program really matters to her," a spokesperson for Winfrey says. "It's not something she just gives money to and leaves to other people." Oprah will be recruiting corporations and individuals to support and help expand the program, "one life, one family at a time. That is how you change the world," said Oprah.

◆ ◆ ◆

One magazine called Stan Curtis "a back-slapping, name-dropping, Cadillac-driving, yuppie stockbroker who has turned the task of feeding the poor into The Greatest Show on Earth." If that's what it takes, it is fine with Stan.

The P. T. Barnum of Philanthropy

Louisville, Kentucky

The early days of Stan Curtis's life were somber ones. Growing up in Louisville, Kentucky, in the 1950's, he was involved in a family crisis that could have easily plunged him, along with his mother and five siblings, into the ranks of the homeless.

Stan's father mistreated the children's mother. As a result, Stan's parents divorced when he was eight. His mother couldn't afford to raise six children, so she placed them in a children's home, and worked there as a house mother.

Stan lived there until he joined the Air

Force. Along the way, he played professional tennis. From 1970 to 1980, he taught tennis. He made such a good living that, at age thirty-one, he was able to retire.

Returning to Kentucky, Stan married a former Miss Louisville and became a stockbroker with J.C. Bradford & Co. For the next few years, he focused on playing golf and making money by making his rich clients richer.

One night in 1987, Stan, then thirty-seven, saw a TV program that changed his life. It featured a report on a food donation network in New York called City Harvest. He wondered why there wasn't a program like it in Louisville.

A few days later, in a cafeteria, Stan saw a server put down a steaming pan filled with green beans and take away a pan that was one-third full. Calling the manager over, Stan asked, "What happens to those leftover beans?"

"We throw them away."

That reply ignited Stan's imagination. Over the next few days, he asked several of his friends, "Do you think we could set up a group of volunteers who would take food from people who have it, but don't want it, and give it to people who want it, but don't have it?"

Before they could reply, Stan answered his own question: "Of course we can!"

With that simple idea, Kentucky Harvest was born.

Stan decided that, unlike the program in New York, his would not ask the public or the government for money. "We're not fund-raising, but food raising," he told prospective volunteers. "You can't send us money and think you're involved. Instead, come and see what's happening among the less fortunate. Use your ideas, talent, and energy to make a difference."

To test his novel idea, Stan set up a pilot program. After two months, Mayor Jerry Abramson made Kentucky Harvest a city program. Soon, a hundred volunteers, driving their own vehicles, were picking up leftover or surplus food from businesses. They would immediately deliver it to missions, where the hungry and homeless came to eat.

By the end of Kentucky Harvest's first year, seventy-three businesses were supplying seventeen missions. In all, 753,000 pounds of food had been salvaged, providing meals for more than ten thousand people. Most of the food was donated by restaurants, hospitals, hotels, bakeries, and caterers.

Stan discovered that Louisville's hungry did not fit the stereotype. A growing number were single parents who worked full-time but did not make enough money to feed their families, one-time business or professional people, or blue-collar workers fallen on hard times. Stan was disturbed that so many children were at the shelters.

Kentucky Harvest was run by volunteers, with no paid staff whatsoever. To oversee the organization, Stan recruited twenty-five board members. Their averge age: thirty-two. They could have written checks that would have been the end of their community involvement. But Stan insisted that they give their time, instead. On one occasion, he actually declined federal government funds.

On January 1, 1989, Kentucky Harvest was featured in Ann Landers's column, nationwide. Stan got 1,100 calls and letters from across the country. People asked, "How can we do this in our town?" By April, twenty cities had set up volunteer organizations modeled on Kentucky Harvest. To provide guidance for the new groups, Kentucky Harvest formed its own parent, U.S.A. Harvest.

In a colorful profile in 1990, *Louisville* magazine described Stan, whose real name is Hugh Vanderbilt Curtis III, as "the P. T. Barnum of philanthropy — a back-slapping, name-dropping, Cadillac-driving yuppie stockbroker who has turned the task of feeding the poor into The Greatest Show on Earth."

Comparing Stan to circus promoter P. T. Barnum was not entirely unfair. After all, Stan had paraded out an elephant to dramatize the huge quantities of food Kentucky Harvest had distributed. Then, to mark its third birthday, he greeted the press in the maw of a Boeing 747 (capacity 110 tons) and asked people to visualize ten such aircraft all packed with nutritious foods. Eleven-hundred and ten tons — more than 2 million pounds — that's how much food Kentucky Harvest had salvaged.

In April 1993, U.S.A. Harvest held its third annual National Hunger Relief Concert, featuring Dolly Parton. Fans were urged to bring a can of food. Those cans, along with 723,000 pounds of food pledged by sponsors, were distributed to eighty-seven cities. Concerts by Van Halen in nineteen cities helped raise 300,000 pounds of food.

Today, at forty-six, Stan is still a stockbroker. But most of his time is devoted to Harvest programs. For Kentucky Harvest, he serves on the board and often helps deliver and serve food. In 1992, the Louisville chapter helped feed nine thousand people a day.

Stan also leads the thirty-seven thousand volunteers of U.S.A. Harvest. During 1992, the national organization, operating in eighty-five cities, gathered nearly fifty million pounds of surplus food. That's enough to fill 228 Boeing 747's.

Says Stan: "I wouldn't quit this work if I won a fifty-million-dollar lottery. I want to give to people. This journey has changed my character," he reflects. "I'm more compassionate. The other day, as I watched homeless kids enjoy a meal they would not have had unless people had cared enough to make it happen, I damn near cried." In 1993, Stan Curtis was honored as one of six recipients of the 1993 America's Awards, presented annually by the Positive Thinking Foundation.

♦ ♦ ♦

Ron Cowart has demonstrated, in the toughest areas of Dallas, that you can create safer communities simply by strengthening families and improving neighborhoods.

Cop Fights Crime with Compassion

Dallas, Texas

As a young boy, Ron Cowart often sat on his father's lap, listening to stories of how Woody Cowart, as a soldier in World War II, had helped save the world. Ron decided then on a simple goal for his life: to fight for good.

At age eighteen, Ron entered the U.S. Navy and volunteered to serve in Vietnam. He wanted to fight Communism. By February 1968, during the Tet offensive, he was doing his part — firing a machine-gun on a patrol boat in the Mekong Delta. He was wounded in one firefight, and received the Purple Heart.

But the satisfaction of victory eluded Ron. In fact, as he got to know the Vietnamese, Ron was shocked. Many of them resented Americans for taking over and tearing up their country and wanted the U.S. soldiers to leave. When his tour was up, Ron left Vietnam disillusioned, hating the Vietnamese for not fighting harder for their country.

Back in Texas, Ron began a career with the Dallas Police Department. During the next few years, he was too busy to think much about Vietnam: while working full-time, he got married, fathered a son, and earned two college degrees.

In May 1974, Ron was assigned to a police tactical squad that, between emergencies, patrolled the areas of the city with the highest crime rates. In the early 1980s, that assignment took him to Little Asia, a square-mile area of East Dallas filled with four thousand refugees from Laos, Cambodia, and Vietnam.

Most of these Southeast Asians were widows and children who had fled their native countries with little more than the clothes on their backs. They had arrived in Dallas penniless and unable to speak English, and had packed themselves into run-down apartment buildings.

Encouraged by his wife, Melinda, a

teacher of English as a second language, Ron started talking to the people in Little Asia. He soon realized that, due to language and cultural barriers, they were not reporting victimization by robbers, drug traders, extortionists, and killers. And they were not aware of resources and how to get the services they needed to survive.

Slowly, Ron began building a bridge between the police and the refugees. That was not an easy task with people who had brought with them a fear of authority. Kids, Ron finally realized, were the key to establishing trust.

So, in December 1983, under sponsorship of the Dallas Police and the Highland Park Baptist Church, where he was a member, Ron founded Explorer Post 68. Its thirty members, all Southeast Asians, began installing peepholes in and safety locks on apartment doors. They also told residents how to protect themselves against crime.

Six months later, Ron had an idea: a storefront where police could earn the people's trust by helping them in their community. He found a suitable location, then persuaded the Meadows Foundation and the police to pool

$160,000 for renovation, utilities, and salaries for three Asian public service officers to assist him. The storefront opened on November 15, 1985.

From day one, Ron was consumed by his new job. He pestered apartment managers to make repairs. Along with his staff, he made daily trips into the community to deliver rice, take kids to school, and the sick to clinics. He coached soccer teams and gave marching and civics lessons to his Explorer Scouts.

Within months, Ron had become Little Asia's pied piper, its hero. Wherever he went, people crowded around him. The bed of his pickup truck usually had at least a half dozen children nestled amid giant bags of rice.

Many of his fellow officers grumbled that policemen have no business being social workers. Ron tried to demonstrate that police can assume both roles. Whenever they called him a bleeding-heart liberal, Ron kidded them back: "It shows I've got a heart to bleed."

With the help of volunteers and donations from private organizations, the storefront distributed electric fans in summer, blankets in winter, and rice all year long. It provided job referrals and mediated domestic problems. It dispensed advice, reassurance, and referrals to other government agencies. It conducted tutoring and sponsored five Boy and Girl Scout troops.

The results were dramatic: fewer crimes, stronger and healthier families, higher rates of employment, and smarter students.

Four times, Ron could have been promoted to police investigator, a position he had longed for. But each time, he turned down the offer. Finally, in July 1989, after four years at the storefront and twenty years as a policeman, Ron Cowart retired. He was forty-one.

The next day, Ron went to work as a crime-prevention manager for the city's Health and Human Services Department. The job, created especially for him, was to duplicate his success by eradicating the roots of crime in *all* of the city's toughest neighborhoods.

In its first year, the Experimental Crime Prevention Program cut crime in the target areas by 17 percent. In the second year, the rate came down an additional 4 percent. The *Dallas Times Herald* hailed the decision to pay Ron to teach people how to fight crime — and city hall — "one of the smartest things the council ever has done."

Today, whenever he looks at the refugee children, Ron wonders, *Did some American soldier give his life for this child?* And he reminds himself: *These kids are not my biological children, but they are still my children.*

At no time has Ron been prouder of "his" children than on July 4, 1990. On that day, twenty-four young people, all members of Explorer Post 111, with whom he had worked, were sworn in as U.S. citizens.

One week later, one of the new citizens, a Laotian refugee named Soulaphonh "Mee" Thammavongsa, left for Marine boot camp. Passing up a college scholarship, Mee explained, "I'm doing this for the Vietnam veterans who fought for our freedom. Becoming a Marine is my way of paying them back."

Ron could hardly hold back the tears. Like so many U.S. soldiers, he had left Vietnam with a sense of a mission unaccomplished. But no more.

A 1992 recipient of the America's Award, Ron Cowart, forty-seven, has demonstrated that law enforcement's best weapon against crime is to earn the trust of the community, and that this is best achieved by helping citizens with their problems.

Few Americans would consider it sacrilegious if the refugees of Little Asia in Dallas were to adopt a new motto for their currency: "In God (and Ron) We Trust."

◆ ◆ ◆

Without his artificial legs, Hank Viscardi stands just three feet eight inches tall. But thousands of people with physical disabilities know him as . . .

A Giant of a Man

Long Island, New York

The son of Italian immigrants, Henry "Hank" Viscardi was born in 1912 with only stumps for legs. He spent the first seven years of his life as a charity patient in the hospital, undergoing painful operations and treatments. Finally, doctors were able to fit his stumps with padded boots. But nothing protected him from people's cruel stares and thoughtless comments.

173

One day, young Hank asked his mother, "Why me?"

In a simple peasant voice, she replied: "When it was time for another crippled boy to be born, the Lord and His councils held a meeting to decide where he should be sent, and the Lord said, 'I think the Viscardis would be a good family to take care of him.'" Hank would hold on to that answer all his life.

Determined to rise above his circumstances, Hank used his quick mind to and dry wit to breeze through primary and high school in New York. So badly did he want to become a "learned man" that he enrolled at Fordham University, working his way through college by sweeping floors and waiting tables. Before leaving Fordham, as an honor student, he was already enrolled in night classes at law school.

Battling the prejudices of others who now towered above his three-foot-eight-inch frame was bad enough. But then his orthopedic surgeon, Dr. Robert Yanover, delivered some devastating news. "Your stumps won't last another six months. You'll probably spend the rest of your life in a wheelchair, unless . . ." Just maybe Hank could be fitted with artificial limbs.

First, there was more surgery. Then, Hank and Dr. Yanover began making the rounds of the artificial-limb makers. Each one said, "Impossible." Finally, a German maker named George Dorsch said, "I can do it."

Two months later, in the fall of 1938, Dorsch helped Hank slip his stumps into the padded sockets of the artificial legs. Then, for the first time in twenty-seven years, Hank stood up straight. Looking in the mirror at his new five-foot-eight-inch profile, he couldn't keep back the tears.

Overwhelmed by the new world his artificial legs had opened to him, Hank went to the doctor who had made it all possible and asked how much he owed. Dr. Yanover replied, "There is no bill. But someday, if you'll make the difference for one other individual, the difference between a life dependent on charity, or life rich with dignity and self-sufficiency, then our account will be squared."

In the years that followed, Hank tried to pay back the doctor many times. After working in a New York tax office, he joined the American Red Cross as a field-service officer. Soon he found himself doing what he had often dreamed of — working with amputees from World War II.

But even artificial limbs did not ease a veteran's passage back into the working world. Many employers considered "cripples" (an unfortunate description at that time of the disabled) a bad risk. So Hank began speaking before business and civic groups as an advocate for the disabled. When several businessmen came up with an innovative pilot program called JOB (Just One Break) designed to find jobs for rehabilitated men and women, they knew there was only one man to run it.

By that time, Hank was married, with the first of his four daughters on the way, and taking the job would require a financial sacrifice. But his wife, Lucile, urged him to accept the challenge. Hank did accept and, as expected, enjoyed great success at placing people with disabilities in responsible jobs.

But the experience only showed him how much more needed to be done. So, in 1952, Hank quit yet another well-paying job, borrowed eight thousand dollars, and founded Abilities, Inc., in a vacant garage. He wanted to prove that, given a chance, the physically handicapped can work effectively in industry.

In the years since, the organization, now known as the National Center for Disability Services, located in Albertson, New York, has gained an international reputation in pioneering the education and rehabilitation of people with disabilities, and has spawned similar programs in sixty countries.

The heart of the center, located on thirteen beautiful acres on Long Island, is the Henry Viscardi School. There, 220 students, ranging in age from prekindergarten through high school, are all physically challenged. Hank created the tuition-free school to provide a place where young people can learn and grow and build a brighter future.

Today, the nonprofit center, supported by state and private funds, operates four units: the school; Abilities Health and Rehabilitation Services, which offers outpatient programs in physical, speech, and occupational therapy, along with psychological services; the Career and Employment Institute, which annually evaluates, trains, and offers job placement to more than six hundred adults with disabilities in computer programming, technical electronics, and secretarial and office work; and the Research and Training Institute.

Now eighty-three years old, Hank is founder of the center. He continues to advise groups and individuals (Although he has not yet had the opportunity to meet with the current resident of the White House, he has advised every other U.S. president since FDR) concerning possibilities for the physically disabled. When he is not receiving an award or giving a speech, he likes to work with students or sail his fifteen-foot sloop near his home on Long Island.

Hank says he would not change any of his life, even the pain and suffering. He cautions young people not to take too seriously the gray days and the sad days that will surely come their way. "They help you reach out to the good things that follow," he says.

Hank believes that both the joyful and the painful moments provide the building blocks for a meaningful life. "You build meaning into your experiences, talents, and out of the things you believe in and the people you love. All of us have the ingredients," he explains, "but we're the only ones who can put them together into that unique pattern that is our lives."

For Hank Viscardi, the faith in God passed on to him from his peasant mother provided one vital ingredient for discovering his own unique pattern. "Without my faith," he says, "my life would have been empty and meaningless. I can't help but believe that the Lord had a plan for my life that made me what I am."

For additional information, please write to: National Center For Disability Services, 201 I.U. Willets Road, Albertson, NY 11507, or call (516) 747-5400.

♦ ♦ ♦

A once-popular book portrayed "The Ugly American." Anne Sweeney's valiant efforts to help thousands of starving, disabled children in the Philippines has created a new stereotype. . . .

The Beautiful American

Woodinville, Washington

Iris Anne Curtner was born into poverty. She entered the world, on May 28,

1937, on a bed of straw. When Anne was five, her parents divorced. Two years later, her father died. She spent much of her childhood with relatives in Arkansas.

While visiting an aunt in California in 1954, Anne met, and soon married, Bill Sweeney. He was an eighteen-year-old Marine.

During her first pregnancy, Anne learned she had bone cancer. Doctors amputated her right leg above the knee and fitted her with a prosthesis. Then, predicting that she had only six months to live, they sent her home to die. God had other plans.

Tragically, the Sweeney's first child died shortly after birth. But Anne and Bill did not let that thwart their efforts to have a large family. They adopted five children. In 1970, after sixteen years of marriage and nine failed pregnancies, Anne gave birth to the first of three children.

In 1984, the couple and their eight children moved to the Philippines, where Bill, then a colonel, commanded the Marine Barracks Security Force at Subic Bay. One day, Bill handed Anne a check for two hundred dollars. An Army chaplain in Illinois had sent it "to help children of Olongapo," a nearby city.

Anne decided to use the money to feed malnourished children. She asked doctors on the base, "How can I give the biggest nutritional boost possible to the most children for the least money?"

With their help, she developed a nutritional "stew" made of chicken, rice, vegetables, and fried beans, as well as a vitamin-enriched milk. By preparing the food herself, Anne managed to feed eighty-six children one meal a week for three months. The cost: twenty-four cents a child a day.

With contributions from Marines, military wives, doctors, and chaplains, Anne was able to expand the program. Soon, she was feeding 450 children from three locations. Gradually, their health began to improve.

Anne Sweeney had found her mission in life: saving lives and providing children who had been rejected by their society — and oftentimes their families — with dignity, hope, and love.

Impressed officials of Olongapo eagerly accepted Anne's offer to administer services to children in the city's malnourished ward. Anne relied on one simple rule: Even if nothing else can be done, every child is to be treated with dignity. Workers were hired and volunteers recruited for their ability to embrace the dirtiest, sickest child, say "I love you," and mean it.

Anne quickly realized that the children were also in desperate need of medical care. Many of them suffered from polio, malaria, or tuberculosis, or had lost their sight or hearing because no aspirin or antibiotics were available to treat high fevers. At her urging, area doctors began providing free medical care.

In 1985, Anne moved the program from her home to a church basement, and named it Children's Hope Center. Soon, the basement also housed a free school for the disabled.

In June 1986, Bill received notice that he was being transferred to San Diego. Because Anne knew she would return to the Philippines often, the impending departure had little emotional effect on her. Instead, she focused on what she was leaving behind: the center at Olongapo, three paid staff members, fifty-four disabled students — and hundreds of grateful children and their families.

As soon as the Sweeneys were settled

at Bill's new duty station, Anna incorporated as the nonprofit International Children's Advocate (ICA).

Supporters were attracted by Anne's refusal to pay herself a salary and by her ability to spend ninety cents of every dollar directly on services. In 1987, for example, ICA provided four hundred handicapped children with 126,000 meals and medical care, including fifty-five surgical procedures, for $40,000 — less than $115 per child.

When Bill retired in 1987, the Sweeneys settled in Woodinville, Washington, near Seattle. Anne didn't retire. She still had four kids to care for at home, including two recent adoptees, which brought to ten the number of Sweeney children.

Seven days a week, many hours a day, Anne worked from home — by phone and letter — to expand ICA. In three years, she returned to the Philippines twelve times, staying an average of two weeks each trip.

By 1991, ICA had opened centers in sixteen additional provinces, and its paid staff numbered fourteen. Donations of cash plus goods in kind totaled nearly $100,000 a year. ICA was serving forty-five hundred kids a year, providing medicines, surgeries, educational and social development, and 166,530 meals.

Then, in June 1991, Anne's dream suffered a terrible blow. Mount Pinatubo erupted, killing hundreds of Filipinos and destroying scores of villages. It also forced ICA to close all seventeen of its survival centers, except the one at Olongapo, the one Anne had started with so long ago.

In December 1992, ICA suffered another serious blow. The United States withdrew from the Philippines all of its troops, ICA's major source of volunteers and contributors. Donations plummeted to $9,900.

But Anne, now fifty-eight, refuses to abandon her goal of establishing a center and school for starving, disabled children in all eighty of the country's provinces.

For motivation, Anne needs only to call up the image of a nine-year-old child with a broken back who had never seen a doctor. For inspiration, she needs only to recall the deaf children who sang to her in sign language. They had much to sing about: their basketball team, the first in the Philippines made up entirely of deaf children, had won an all-province championship.

Once hidden, starving, and ashamed, the children Anne has worked with now shine with new-found health, pride in themselves and their accomplishments, and community acceptance.

Thousands of children have been touched, hundreds of lives saved, and most changed forever, because Anne Sweeney has steadfastly acted on her simple conviction: "If I know something is wrong and I have the ability to change it, I have the responsibility to act with love."

◆ ◆ ◆

For over a year, organizers of a bold project to help patients with Alzheimer's in South Carolina have marveled at how effective — and simple — the treatment is. It provides a chance for patients to relive their playfulness from another time, with spontaneous and joyful visits with another generation, and that is how . . .

Affection of Toddlers Helps Alzheimer's Patients Become Caregivers Again

Columbia, South Carolina

When a group of preschoolers sang, "Thanksgiving Day is coming, so Mr. Turkey said, 'How careful I must be or I shall lose my head,' " to a group of visitors to the R Kids Only day-care center in Columbia, South Carolina, beaming and clapping along with them was Eunice Perry, an eighty-seven-year-old Hamilton House Nursing Center resident who had Alzheimer's disease.

A few minutes earlier, Perry had said she didn't want to come along and, in a van coming to the childcare center, had accused nursing home workers of trying to harm her.

The children continued, "The pumpkin told the turkey, 'How frightened, too, am I. They'll mix me up with sugar and spice, and I'll be pumpkin pie.' "

Perry was visiting the children along with three other women from the nursing home: Gabriella Rodriguez, Opie Davis, and Marguerite Ramsey.

All of the women were in early stages of Alzheimer's, a progressive, degenerative disease that attacks the brain and results in impaired memory, thinking, and behavior. An estimated four million

Americans have Alzheimer's.

Before their visit, the women seemed helpless and childlike — using crayons to color pictures at tables in the nursing home's activity room. Once surrounded by children, the women swiftly turned into care givers.

Accompanied by Margarita Jara, Hamilton House's social services director, and Tana Strain, director of R Kids Only, the women made their way through the center with apparent ease. They "oohed" and "aahed" and clucked over the children like doting grandmothers.

"Where are the babies?" Rodriguez asked as she walked in the door. Rodriguez later spoke in Spanish to the babies.

Someone asked Davis, "Miss Opie, what have you got?" She answered, "I don't know, about ten pounds."

In one baby room, Davis told a baby, "You've got a bad cold," and then exclaimed, "I'd love to take every one of them." She calmed a fussy baby by rocking him for several minutes.

The biggest change, however, seemed to take place in Perry, the woman who had resisted coming along that morning.

She moved from the preschooler area to a baby room, standing and clapping, at times bending over to talk to a child before settling into a rocking chair where she had become a magnet for the babies.

"You can't stand up," she teased one baby. "That baby doesn't know what he's doing. He can't even talk," she said to no one in particular.

She smiled and laughed throughout her thirty minutes or so in a room full of babies, some crawling and a few walking. "I've seen you before," she told one baby.

"Look at there. Look at his britches. He's got on shoes," Perry said.

Seated in her rocking chair, she scooped ten-month-old Julie Glass off the floor and onto her lap. Though at times it was hard to make out what Perry was saying and singing, she kept a patter going.

Though absorbed with the baby in her lap, Perry noticed others, too. She noticed one who was crawling around her feet. When told that a baby was behind her chair, she stopped rocking until the way was cleared.

"Who's that?" she asked when a baby

cried elsewhere in the room. "Don't let that baby fall down," she instructed others.

When the baby girl in her lap grabbed Perry's necklace, she said, "I love you. Go right on."

What went on that day was remarkable to visitors, but those involved have seen it happen once or twice a week for months. Organizers hope the project will spread as a cost-effective, humane, and enjoyable way to help people with Alzheimer's and their caregivers.

In its early stages, Alzheimer's causes memory loss of things that have just occurred, confusion, and shortened attention spans.

By the end stage, victims of the disease can't recognize family members or themselves in the mirror, often lose weight, have little capacity for self-care, can't communicate with words, can't control bowels and bladder, may put everything into their mouth or touch everything, and may have seizures, according to Alzheimer's Association materials.

For many patients, though, the daycare visits provide a chance to step back in time, relying on childcare skills and playfulness from another time.

It suits many of their tendencies — walking around, reacting emotionally, showing affection — and helps dissipate the restless energy often associated with Alzheimer's.

"Me and you. Ha, ha, ha," Eunice Perry sang to the baby, who responded by smiling and cooing back at her, and sitting calmly in her lap. "Jack and Jill went up that hill . . . Come and see me . . . Cutest little baby I've ever seen." The eighty-seven-year-old woman's smile lit up the room.

♦ ♦ ♦

Do you have a special skill or interest that could benefit others in need? In addition to the organizations that are seeking volunteers in the preceding stories, there are many others. Parade *magazine's Washington Bureau Chief Jack Anderson lists a few that could use your help.*

Volunteer — It Can Enrich Your Life

Volunteer service has never been more popular than today. *Parade* magazine, for a special issue in 1995, scoured the federal bureaucracy to find some of the interesting ways individuals could help their government and country in their spare time. Here are a few:

- **Students can help out — while earning money for school.** This year, up to twenty thousand Americans aged seventeen or older are taking part in AmeriCorps. In exchange for work in rural or urban communities for one or two years, they will receive education vouchers of $4,725 per year for college or vocational training. Members also receive a living stipend as well as health insurance. AmeriCorps members clean up neighborhoods, police the streets, build houses for the homeless, tutor children, and more. For information, call: (800) 94-ACORP.

- **Are you good with numbers?** How about helping people with their tax returns? Through Volunteer Income Tax Assistance or Tax Counseling for the Elderly, you'll get free training from the Internal Revenue Service (which also might help with your own return). As an IRS volunteer, you'll help the disabled, the elderly, and lower-income taxpayers. To find out about training programs, call the IRS information helpline at (800) 829-1040.

- **Do you have a little time to spare?** Those aged fifty-five or older are eligible for the Retired and Senior Volunteer Program, to work in libraries, police stations, hospitals, and homeless shelters. Call the National Senior Service Corps at: (800) 424-8867.

- **Navigate tourists around the Smithsonian**. In our nation's capital and in New York, many volunteers serve as information specialists and tour guides at the Smithsonian's sixteen museums and the National Zoo. For information, write to Smithsonian Information, Dept. P, SI Building, Room 153, MRC 010, Washington, D.C. 20560; or call (202) 357-2700.

- **Curious about science?** Volunteers of all ages can help scientists and experts at the U.S. Geological Survey, the nation's largest earth science research organization. Volunteers gather water quality data, survey ore deposits, update maps, monitor earthquake and volcanic activity, and work with the latest computer technology. The U.S. Geological Survey staff members provide training as needed. To find out about the Volunteer for Science program, write USGS, Dept. P, 601 National Center, Reston, VA 22092; or call (703) 648-7440.

- **Lend a hand and breathe *fresh air*.** If you think you'd like to band birds at a wildlife refuge, raise fish at a fish hatchery, or conduct wildlife surveys, then consider volunteering with the Fish and Wildlife Service, which has more than six hundred field stations. Write to Volunteer Coordinator, U.S. Fish and Wildlife Service, Dept. P, 4401 Fairfax Drive, Room 670, Arlington, VA 22203.

- **Brighten a veteran's day.** At the

193

Veterans Affairs (VA) medical centers, volunteers escort patients, read and write letters, teach crafts, and assist with administrative work. Interested? Contact the chief of voluntary service at the VA medical center or outpatient clinic in your area. It's listed in the telephone directory under U.S. Government.

- **Do you like to work with children?** If you do, a Head Start center has a place where you can help. The federal social and educational program is for children in low-income families and is operated in urban and rural areas. Volunteers have acted as translators, given puppet shows, worked in classrooms, cooked, tutored, and helped plant gardens. For more information, write Head Start Bureau, Dept. P, P.O. Box 1182, Washington, D.C. 20013.

- **Help the elderly.** The Administration on Aging, created by the Older Americans Act, provides a range of services to the elderly. Volunteers investigate complaints of nursing home residents, deliver meals, provide counseling, and escort people to medical appointments. To find out which agency in your area may offer volunteer programs, call the Administration on Aging's Elderly Locator at (800) 677-1116.

CHAPTER 6

CORPORATIONS *DO* HAVE HEARTS

From what we get, we can make a living. What we give, however, makes a life.

—Arthur Ashe

Big businesses, like politicians, too often have an image problem. In major news stories of oil spills, layoffs, factory closings, and leveraged buyouts, in television dramas and countless films, corporations and business leaders are cast as greedy, heartless villains. Yet their contributions to America's well-being and their humanitarian deeds usually go unheralded. The stories selected here are inspirational examples of businesses and business people whose bottom line includes caring, compassion, and contributing.

◆ ◆ ◆

*When restaurateur George MacLeod
was forced to drop his employee health
insurance because costs had quadrupled, he knew he had to figure out a way
to reinstate the insurance without going
broke. His novel solution could be a
model for thousands of businesses.*

Meals for Medical Insurance

Bucksport, Maine

A pair of red tugboats maneuvers an
oil tanker under a bridge, a cloud of
steam rises from a paper mill's smoke-
stacks, and logging trucks rumble down
icy Main Street. The small town seems
an unlikely place for cutting-edge health
care programs. But restaurant owner
George MacLeod thinks he may have hit
on a model plan for a nation with thirty-
seven million uninsured people.

One Sunday each month, MacLeod's
Restaurant is turned over to the employees. The money they make is used to pay
for their health insurance, and they get
to keep any extra profits.

"What we've done here is hit upon a

solution that works for us. Small businesses do this all the time. We're constantly forced to reassess to solve our problems," said MacLeod, sitting in an office over his business.

The eighty-five-seat restaurant where the idea was hatched has paneled walls adorned with pictures of tugs and other working boats that once filled the Penobscot River. The menu is a blend of meat and potatoes, fresh fish, pasta dishes, and barbecued ribs.

Floor manager Kathy Shissler said the employees don't mind an extra day of cooking, serving, and cleaning if it means they have health coverage. "I don't like to take the chance because if I ever get sick, I might lose everything," Shissler said. "I have a chance here to work for my insurance. It's an important factor to me."

Seven workers who might not have had health coverage are now insured because of the First Sunday program, MacLeod said. Eight other workers have health insurance through their spouses.

MacLeod dropped his insurance plan in the late 1980s after the cost jumped from about $25 a month to more than

$100 a month over seven years.

It was a troubling decision for MacLeod, who found himself personally buying eyeglasses for one worker, putting another through a substance abuse program, and getting orthopedic shoes for yet another.

He knew he needed to figure out a way to reinstate the insurance without going broke. Now it costs an average of about $130 a month per employee, he said. He considered a surcharge on meals and other options before coming up with the idea of letting employees open the restaurant on a day when it's normally closed.

It works like this: Employees do the planning and MacLeod provides the free use of his restaurant. Workers use 7 percent of their revenues to pay sales tax and another 35 percent to pay for the food. They use the rest to pay for health insurance, and any remaining profits after payroll taxes are pooled together and divided among the employees.

There is an incentive to be creative: if the employees don't make enough money to cover everything, the shortfall comes out of their paychecks. So far, the program has been a hit among residents. With most places closed Sundays, the restaurant attracts about a hundred customers for each First Sunday, MacLeod said. The revenues are about $1,200 each month, he said.

To keep the customers coming, the employees plan themes, such as Italian food one month, and bands to entertain customers another. Jeff Prince, senior director of the 150,000-establishment National Restaurant Association, said most workers in the restaurant industry don't have, or expect, health insurance.

"What a great idea," said Prince, adding that many restaurants can't afford the costs of insurance because of declining profit margins.

MacLeod thinks his idea could work for others: a manufacturer, for example, could dedicate proceeds from a particular product line to provide insurance. Businesses should come up with their own creative solutions because the health care problem is too broad to be solved by government alone, he said. "Our ability as a nation to deal with the problem depends on the creativity of individuals."

♦ ♦ ♦

Raymond Dunn, Jr., was born with a broken skull and a brain that had been deprived of oxygen; he was not supposed to live a year. He suffered up to two dozen seizures a day and slept two to three hours a night. His biggest problem was his allergies to virtually all food . . . except a product called MBF, made by Gerber, the baby food company. Raymond died in January 1995, at the age of twenty, his life prolonged by the generosity of a giant corporation and its employees.

The "Gerber Boy"

The Catskills, New York

For all of his twenty years, Raymond Dunn, Jr., of New York couldn't walk or talk — in fact, he could barely breathe. But Raymond could do one thing. He could make people care.

His mother and father dedicated their lives to him. Strangers offered their help and their love. And a big corporation gave him sustenance.

Raymond was known as the "Gerber Boy" because just for him the company resumed production of a discontinued infant formula — the only food to which the profoundly retarded young man was not allergic.

He died in January 1995 in a hospital near his home in the Catskills, ending a life no less valued for all its troubles. "He fought right up to the end. He wanted so much to stay with us," his mother, Carol Dunn, said Thursday. "But he suffered all his life, especially at the end. He racked his little body, just trying to breathe."

When he died, the Dunns still had a year's supply of a brownish liquid called MBF (for meat-based formula). Gerber stopped making it in 1985, but employee volunteers of Gerber retooled five years later after hearing that Raymond's doctors said he would die without it.

"Gerber says, 'Babies are our business,' but Raymond's their business, too," said Carol Dunn. By 1988 Mrs. Dunn had hunted down every can of the now discontinued MBF she could find and Gerber had exhausted its backlog. The mother begged Gerber to make more.

Finally, in 1990, the company agreed. Research division volunteers put their own projects on hold, hauled out old equipment, and devoted several thousand square feet and several days of production time and space to Raymond's MBF. They even had to go to Washington to get USDA approval for the label.

The special batch was meant to last two years. When Raymond finished it, Gerber made more; when he died, he still had a year's supply. The story of the corporate heart stirred many others. Mrs. Dunn and her husband, Raymond, Sr., a car salesman, got sacks of mail. A Sunday school class sent twenty-eight dollars. A dealer in rare baseball cards offered Raymond any one he wanted. A man in Skokie, Illinois, informally adopted Raymond as his grandson.

A Gerber nutritionist, Dr. Sandra Bartholmey, seemed surprised when asked why she and her colleagues devoted such effort to a market of one. "It seemed like the right thing to do," she said.

Now, his mother said, she will devote the energy she once put into her son's care to raise money to build the Raymond Dunn Rainbow House, a facility for "medically fragile, technology-dependent children." "Families in this situation need help," she said. "You have no idea of what it's like before you get there."

Gerber knew, they understood, and they acted. Because they did, Raymond Dunn had nineteen more years of life than the doctors had predicted at his birth.

◆ ◆ ◆

Hyatt Hotels has always been a socially conscious company, participating in the community through various programs, encouraging its individual employees' volunteerism by giving them paid time off to serve, and treating its employees as family. When Darryl Hartley-Leonard became Hyatt's President in 1986, that corporate philosophy was enhanced.

For Hyatt Chairman — Caring Is the Key!

Chicago, Illinois

"All of us must get involved. The future is of our economy and our country depends on it." Few adhered to those words of Darryl Hartley-Leonard more closely than Hartley-Leonard himself.

The Chairman of Hyatt Hotels Corporation has applied his philosophy of getting involved in all aspects of work. Having worked for Hyatt since 1964, becoming president in 1986, and Chairman in 1994, Hartley-Leonard, 52, is so familiar with the company that the programs he has enacted that get him and his employees involved seem a natural outgrowth of the man and the company.

As part of his drive to get everyone involved, Hartley-Leonard also launched Hyatt's Family of Responsible and Caring Employees (FORCE). Every manager who works with Hyatt receives four paid days a year to volunteer in the community.

For example, in Scottsdale, Arizona, managers volunteer at a sexual and physical abuse victim's center. Managers in New Orleans translate cookbooks and restaurant menus into Braille at the Lighthouse for the Blind. Staffers in San Francisco sweep the streets every Wednesday.

Hartley-Leonard estimates that in a given month, about 1,000 Hyatt employees are out in the community — getting involved.

The Hyatt Chairman believes that education is one of the most important things to get involved in. He quotes the following figures: In 1986, school dropouts cost the economy an estimated $147 billion. Productivity losses caused by poorly trained workers cost approximately $25 billion annually. It makes sense for business to get involved in education.

Hyatt is doing so with alacrity in Chicago. At the Roberto Clemente Community Academy, Hyatt gave $500,000 to design and build a kitchen and sends its cook over to the school several times a week to teach students marketable job skills in food preparation. The goal of this program is twofold: give students a reason to stay in school, and give them skills that will enable them to apply for jobs. Each summer Hyatt hires 10 interns from the school; more than 300 students are enrolled in the program.

"If you can hook these kids at 14 or 15," Hartley-Leonard says, "you can really make a difference, and that's what we aim to do."

Hartley-Leonard has Hyatt involved in

the communities in many ways. As part of a pilot program, Hyatt took a homeless person off the streets and trained him for a hotel industry post.

Many Hyatt hotels are involved in Adopt-a-School programs, and Hyatt has pledged $250,000 to the American Hotel Foundation, the scholarship subsidiary of the American Hotel and Motel Association, to benefit students seeking degrees in hotel management. Hyatt has also introduced a minority summer internship program.

The Wall Street Journal selected Hyatt as one of only 66 firms worldwide "poised to make a difference in the industries and markets of the 1990's and beyond."

"We have a philosophy that says we're going to take care of people whether they like it or not, and we keep on saying it over and over again and have done so for 20 years," declares Hartley-Leonard.

Under Hartley-Leonard's leadership, people find that they want to work for such a socially conscious company. Hartley-Leonard instituted Hyatt In Touch Day as part of the In Touch for the 90's quality assurance program at Hyatt. On this day, Hyatt executive office staff go out onto the front line. On the first Hyatt In Touch Day, the Hyatt chief was a doorman, and his fellow doormen were impressed by his willingness and good humor. What did Hartley-Leonard get out of it — besides tips? It was a chance for "the chiefs to get in touch with their Indians." He hopes the corporate staff will learn through this annual event that "their function in life is to support the field."

Some Hyatt employees are big beneficiaries of the policy of involvement with staffers. Any employee who has a rock-solid business idea can get it funded by Hyatt. For example, when Hyatt couldn't find the type of diver operator that could handle all its business, Hyatt funded a diving equipment and catamaran rental company called Red Sail, which now works for Hyatt and other companies.

A sales manager for Hyatt approached Hartley-Leonard with a "right-on idea" — Hartley-Leonard teamed him up with Hyatt's financial officer and gave him a $750,000 startup loan. Exactly one year later, that new company turned a $125,000 profit.

"That's the way we think around here," Hartley-Leonard says. "Seize the opportunity. We treat all of our employees as businesspeople."

But the company also treats its employees as family. "Yes, it's family," the Chairman says. "It's affection. It's having the guts to show affection, to tell people you like them or tell people you love them, or giving them a hug. That's motivating to me."

Hartley-Leonard has learned as he moved up in the Hyatt Hotels Corporation, and particularly from the man who hired him almost 32 years ago, that there is no reason to treat people poorly.

Pat Foley was general manager of a Hyatt in southern California when Darryl Hartley-Leonard found himself destitute and in need of a job. He went up to the desk clerk in that Hyatt hotel and asked whether they were taking job applications. Someone made a derogatory comment about his "Limey accent," and Foley came out from his office and began to talk. "And he was of Irish heritage, so we joked about that," remembers Hartley-Leonard. "He asked me what I was doing and I explained it and sure enough, he offered me a job."

Foley asked Hartley-Leonard how he would get to work and, on hearing that the young man would take the bus, as he had no car, Foley took him by the arm and went across the street to a bank to co-sign for an $800 car loan. "That probably was the most significant thing — probably if I look back on all the things that happened — that framed how I approach employees." Foley taught him that "once you have power you give up the right to abuse people."

Pat Foley was one of the most influential people in Hartley-Leonard's life, and this lesson was well taken in both his business and family life.

Well respected, the Chairman of Hyatt is described as having vision and values. Hartley-Leonard has two children, a daughter and a son. "When I am with them, I lose all track of everything else. They are the greatest therapy."

That's not to say that he doesn't try to instill in them some of his own values. Education is paramount in importance, as is family. "You can never abuse your mother," he has told his children, and it is the only thing that he will let them see him lose his temper about. "You're going to have a reverence for something, and she symbolizes the reverence for family, and they know it." He goes to great pains to provide a good example at home as well as within the office. "It's the value of the family unit — it's the only stability that we have."

Hartley-Leonard would also advise kids on balance in life. "The balance would be the effort that you put into community and the effort that you put into self. Work like heck. Work hard, try to be successful, try to succeed, try to do a little more than the person next to you. But as the balance to that, give the same amount of your human resource effort to the community, because community is the material resource of business." Evidence of his belief is in the FORCE program that he created through Hyatt.

The strength of the country, he believes, is going to be in the community. "That's what's going to make us an economic powerhouse." But the economy of the country will also depend on the youth of today getting an education. His efforts through Hyatt speak to the importance of that belief. "I am just consumed by that issue, because I think it is our country's Achilles heel in a global economy of the next century."

No one can overestimate, in Hartley-

Leonard's opinion, how grave the circumstances are within American business. "If you take individual corporations, America is an adolescent country, and America therefore brings with it the personality of all adolescents. Adolescents are greedy, selfish, creative, wonderful, exciting, short-term thinkers . . . What can drag you off center is indeed that short-term thinking — profit-now, gotta-have-it-now, failing-if-it-isn't-now, no-time-to-build-for-the-future thinking."

The attendant fear of American corporations is that they will not be part of an American economic powerhouse in the future — that they won't be competitive because of educational problems. So Hartley-Leonard stresses education to youth, but not to the exclusion of community. He comes back to that value of balance.

The bottom line for young people, he says, is "to get on with it. Get out there and put the same amount of energy that you do into your careers into your community, because it's the only hope we've got.

"I really do believe that the hope for the future of the world is in children; it's not in adults . . . So when I started to get into a position with some clout in community or with a corporation, I decided the focus would be children."

Hartley-Leonard is on the board of directors of the U.S. Committee for UNICEF and is chairman for its fundraising committee. He also serves as a board member of Youth Guidance, a nonprofit social services agency serving Chicago's youth, and the Big Shoulders Fund, a program to support the Catholic schools of Chicago.

"UNICEF I think is the epitome of [this perspective]," Hartley-Leonard speculates. "They do so much with so little . . . So I think to myself, 'If I've got a little clout and a little influence and a lot of energy, maybe we can just make it a little bit better.' Now is that idealism, apple pie, motherhood? . . . Yes, I guess it is all of those things, but it's me."

Hartley-Leonard had a difficult upbringing to shape his adulthood. His mother raised him alone. She had come from a wealthy family that lost its wealth in the Depression. "Suddenly she found herself the daughter of a mother and father who were ill equipped to run a fish-and-chips shop that they bought."

She went on to marry, but when Hartley-Leonard's father didn't come back from World War II, she raised her son alone. "She became a nurse's aide, and a waitress, and a lot of other things in life. The good fortune that I had was that I got to go to a good school. She was determined to do that, and I got to go as a hardship case to a school up in Lancashire, England."

Hartley-Leonard remembers that his mother worked for seven pounds a week. She would save a portion of money so that "at least once every three months she could take me out to dinner and show me the way people ate . . . I've never forgotten those experiences."

He remembers that once they did not have anywhere to live and were on the road for two or three days. "I remember one particular stretch of road. We're walking up a hill, and she gave me a piece of chocolate and said, 'Now you make that last because that's the last piece we have.' You talk about divine intervention: it was about two hours later that she got a job."

The way he was brought up, he says, "gave me great resilience." That resilience shows in the advice he would give to senior citizens.

"The advice I'd wish to give seniors is, 'Fight for your rightful place in life. You earned it, and what you've got to give, if it isn't accepted freely, force it on us, because we'll learn a lot.'"

Hartley-Leonard feels that emotionally society discards the aging population and the wisdom they have gained. Thus the elderly have "abdicated their responsibility to society to some extent." He would urge them to take that responsibility back, to again be involved in society.

Hartley-Leonard sees the links in the future between children, education, community involvement, and the well-being of the world. His bottom line through it all is, "In the end, do what's right." And by doing that he will certainly be remembered the way he would like to be — as a player, as involved, and making a difference.

—By Val J. Halamandaris
Reprinted with permission of
Caring People Magazine, Val J. Halmandaris, Publisher.

◆ ◆ ◆

The Business Enterprise Trust was founded in 1989 by Norman Lear, Chairman of ACT III Communications, along with seventeen other leaders in American business, labor, media, and academia. This nonprofit organization seeks to shine a spotlight on acts of courage, integrity, and social vision in business. Since 1991, the Trust has conferred the annual Business Enterprise Awards on selected business people and firms whose behavior advances the compelling principle that businesses that serve their constituencies in creative and morally thoughtful ways also serve their shareholders best in the long run. The following four profiles are about businesses and individuals who are recipients of the Business Enterprise Award, and were provided by the Business Enterprise Trust for use in this book. Information about BET may be obtained by writing: BET, 204 Junipero Serra Blvd., Stanford, CA 94305.

♦ ♦ ♦

GE Plastics routinely sponsored em-
ployee golf and tennis matches and other
physical competitions as a means of fos-
tering teamwork and improving morale.
In 1988, the company's general desire for
team building gained a new urgency. GE
acquired Borg-Warner Chemicals, which
meant the integration of five thousand
new employees with GE's existing nine
thousand — two groups that had been
arch rivals for decades. How could GE
Plastics cultivate trust and loyalty
among former Borg-Warner employees,
"re-recruit" its own existing employees,
and deal with the emotional trauma of
staff layoffs and restructuring resulting
from the acquisition? The solution it
came up with did more than this 1991
Business Enterprise Award winner ex-
pected.

Corporate Teamwork Rebuilds Communities

San Diego, California

GE Plastics devised a remarkably simple but creative plan to combine employee team building with community

service. Instead of their usual golf, tennis, and other employee competitions, the sales, marketing technology, and manufacturing departments of GE Plastics took a day out of their 1989 national meetings to renovate needy community facilities in San Diego, California. This program, called "Share to Gain," proved exceptionally successful at fostering team spirit while leaving something meaningful behind for the people of San Diego.

Joel Hutt, GE Plastics' manager of marketing communications, first proposed the "Share to Gain" concept. With the enthusiastic encouragement of GE Management, Hutt and a small team spent several months planning renovation projects near the national meeting site. Extensive planning was necessary to select suitable projects and to ensure that hundreds of GE employees could simply walk onto the sites and be effective. At the national meetings, employees were divided into work groups and asked to attend short "skills sessions" to get some basic training in painting, tile-laying, etc. Hutt received tremendous response: about 99 percent of the workforce participated. In total, the four GE

Plastics departments renovated five San Diego community facilities including three YMCA buildings, a boys' and girls' club, and a shelter for the homeless. Over the two weeks of meetings, 3,200 gallons of paint were applied, 2,000 windows installed, and over 40,000 square feet of vinyl and carpet laid.

In addition to making a profound impact on the community centers, GE Plastics gives glowing reports on the team building effects of "Share to Gain." Prior to the San Diego meetings, many managers from Borg-Warner still considered GE Plastics to be "the competition." After a day of pounding nails, painting walls, and planting shrubs, they were teammates. The success of the experiment has led GE to replicate the project elsewhere within the company and to promote the concept to other organizations.

◆ ◆ ◆

If you are a newcomer in the direct mail marketing business, and you want to emphasize the quality of your merchandise as well as give something back to your community, how do you go about it?

That was the challenge Gun Denhart of Hanna Andersson took on.

"Hannadowns" for Kids

Hanna Andersson is a direct mail order marketer of 100% cotton clothing, established by Gun Denhart and her husband, Tom. Upon the birth of their son in 1980, the Denharts had trouble finding durable, attractive cotton clothing for children — the type Gun wore as a girl in her native Sweden. Feeling there was an opportunity to capitalize on the second generation of the Baby Boom, the couple in 1983 began what would quickly become a successful mail order company.

Gun Denhart conceived of the "Hannadowns" program in 1986 during a conversation with a friend who had commented on the waste tolerated in the U.S. as compared to Sweden. For marketing purposes, Denhart wanted to emphasize the durability of the clothes — the idea that "Hannas" are made to last for more than one child.

For social purposes, she wanted to somehow give back to the community that supported her business, particularly to those less fortunate. These multiple goals resulted in Hannadowns, a program which encourages Hanna Andersson customers to return their used clothing for a 20 percent credit on future purchases.

The company then donates the clothes to needy children, in particular those living in emergency shelters to escape abuse, and to those who are homeless. As of March 1994, the Hannadowns promotion has generated credits of over $700,000. The program continues to grow rapidly. The Hannadowns program is a key feature of the marketing strategy which has seen the company grow to over 600,000 customers, 270 employees and annual sales of over $44 million. The company sends out 13 million catalogues per year.

Hannadowns is the cornerstone of a broader commitment on the part of Gun Denhart to support programs specifically geared to disadvantaged women and children. Now that Hanna Andersson is a commercial success, Denhart, a 1992 recipient of the Business Enterprise Award, continues to explore ways to support social change while enhancing her company's business success.

♦ ♦ ♦

A researcher for Merck & Company, Inc., thought one of his company's veterinary drugs could treat an ancient disease called river blindness that affects over eighteen million people in Africa, parts of Latin America, and the Middle East. Because of the poverty of the disease's victims, there was virtually no commercial reward for developing it. But they did it anyway.

A Large Dose of Compassion

It is estimated that 18 million people in Africa and parts of Latin America and the Middle East carry parasitic worms that cause the painful, debilitating disease of onchocerciasis, commonly known as river blindness. Hordes of Microfilariae swarm through the victims' skin and eyes, causing extremely severe itching, skin decay, lesions in the eyes, and eventual blindness. Some 350,000 of those afflicted are currently blind.

The first sign that there might be a preventive drug treatment for this ancient disease came in the late 1970's, when Merck researcher Will Campbell suggested that the river blindness parasite could be neutralized by a Merck Veterinary drug, ivermectin. From the start, Merck realized that the potential commercial market for a treatment was dubious, given the poverty of the disease's victims. Nonetheless, the company, led by Dr. P. Roy Vagelos, the head of Merck's research division and now Chairman and CEO, gave the go-ahead for further research. By 1985, human clinical tests demonstrated that the drug, later named Mectizan, was safe for human use and remarkably effective at just a single dose per year. The French government approved Mectizan for use against onchocerciasis in October 1987.

Neither host governments nor international health organizations, however, could shoulder the costs of producing Mectizan. Furthermore, simply giving the drug away was not a solution because no distribution system existed to reach the millions of potential victims in isolated rural areas. Pressed by the realization that any delay would cost thousands of lives, Merck decided not only to donate an unlimited supply of Mectizan to the estimated 18 million at-risk individuals, but to help create a reliable international apparatus for distributing the drug.

Merck convened a five-member expert committee of world-class scientists and health officials to devise medical protocols for the safe distribution, record keeping and monitoring of Mectizan. The company has also played a major role in informing governments of the drug's existence and value, assigning a full-time "product manager" to oversee distribution, and creating a medical liaison with recipient African nations. Thanks to Merck's ongoing commitment, as of the end of 1993, over seven million persons have been treated in on-going programs in 34 countries. Merck was awarded one of the 1992 Business Enterprise Awards for this significant act of social conscience and business leadership.

◆ ◆ ◆

Life insurance. A benefit payable only upon death. For the terminally ill or those confined to nursing homes whose assets and savings, and often those of their loved one, are wiped out prior to death, it doesn't help. Prudential Insurance came up with a better idea:

Life Insurance for the Living

The aging of the population and increasing costs of terminal illness are placing intense new burdens on the nation's system of long-term health care. Nursing home costs are skyrocketing, and more than 10 percent of elderly Americans require such care today — a number certain to climb in the decades ahead.

In January 1990, Prudential announced an innovative approach to coping with spiraling costs: a new "Living Needs Benefit" option offered, at no additional charge, to their life insurance policyholders. The option, which allows the terminally ill and permanently confined to receive life insurance benefits *before* their death, creates a brand of life insurance that is both humane and cost-effective. By giving the terminally ill access to what is frequently their only major asset, the program can provide some dignity and control in the final months of life.

The concept of accelerated benefits

was first considered by Prudential employees in both the United States and Canada in 1986. That year, Ron Barbaro, at the time President of Prudential's Canadian operation, visited a Toronto AIDS hospice. Moved by a patient's plea to "help us die with dignity," Barbaro charged his employees with developing a way in which terminally ill and permanently confined policyholders could gain earlier access to their benefits.

Despite initial concerns that it was not feasible, the group eventually developed the product. Concurrently, Prudential attorneys and actuaries in the United States were discussing alternate designs for their own "accelerated benefit" rider and the substantial legal and regulatory hurdles such a program would encounter. While Barbaro had an easier time instituting the rider in Canada, Prudential employees in the U.S. labored through an excruciating year-and-a-half process of regulatory and legislative approval of the program in each of the fifty states.

The program pays approximately 90-95 percent of the face value of the policy. There is no upfront charge: rather, it is "paid" by applying a discount rate to the benefit, if and when the accelerated benefit is requested. Claims are processed within two weeks, and there are absolutely no restrictions on how the insured may use the benefit. As of October 1993, Prudential had paid out more than $48 million to 588 policyholders, with an average payout of over $80,000.

Since Prudential took the lead, many other insurance companies have followed suit in offering some form of accelerated benefits. Prudential's business has benefitted as well: increase sales of Prudential's permanent life policies is in part attributed to agent and customer interest in accelerated benefit riders. Prudential officials also report the program has significantly boosted company morale. For their sensitivity to the needs of its policyholders in creating the innovative Living Needs Benefits program, Prudential was honored with The Business Enterprise Award in 1992.

♦ ♦ ♦

You probably haven't heard of Raymond Chambers. He is one of the richest men in America, but he shuns publicity, particularly when he is . . .

Giving Millions Back

Newark, New Jersey

Raymond Chambers once earned more than $100 million in a single leveraged buyout. Yet, over the past several years, one of the nation's wealthiest men has devoted himself full time to rebuilding his hometown of Newark, N.J. Avoiding publicity, he has spent more than $50 million of his own money, and committed another $36 million in the form of bank guarantees to show how philanthropy and business tactics can effectively work together.

The son of an office manager, Chambers, 51, watched Newark lose one-third of its population in the years following bloody riots in 1967. Today, of the remaining 275,000 residents — 85 percent black and Hispanic — more than one in four live in poverty. "I had never seen people as down and out as the people of Newark," says Chambers. "It had got so bad, I didn't think I had an alternative."

In 1988, he left the business world and

waded in. Through his Amelior Foundation, of which he is chairman, Chambers first targeted four dilapidated facilities owned by the Boys' and Girls' Clubs of Newark. He attracted an influential board and quadrupled the clubs' budget. Within 18 months he'd restored the clubs to mint condition and provided a haven for 5,000 new members.

No bank would loan money to build a cinema in Newark's most blighted neighborhood, the Central Ward. But Chambers's foundation put up some funds and then persuaded Loews Theatre management to run the movie house at cost, with the profits going to the city and to civic and cultural activities in the vicinity.

Newark's school system wasn't working either. So Chambers endowed 650 grade-school and junior high students with $10 million for tutoring and parental assistance, as well as for future college costs. As a more immediate incentive, Chambers's foundation bought a stake in a local minority-owned bank and set aside $500 worth of shares for each child to "inherit" upon graduation from high school. The shares help the kids, and the capital infusion helped the bank continue to make loans in inner-city Newark.

"I deal with thousands of people who have money and want to help the city," says Newark Mayor Sharpe James. "But Ray is unique. He doesn't say you must do this and that, and he never asks for anything in return."

—Reprinted by permission of *The Wall Street Journal*, Copyright 1992, Dow Jones & Company, Inc. All Rights Reserved Worldwide.

◆ ◆ ◆

To celebrate its seventy-fifth year in business, KLM Royal Dutch Airlines decided to do something that would celebrate the human spirit.

"Bridging the World"

New York, New York

KLM's seventy-fifth anniversary theme, "Bridging the World," underscores the vision of its founder, Albert Plesman, that "the air ocean unites all peoples." Under this theme, KLM decided to help fulfill long-cherished dreams and ideals through air travel. People from all over the world were invited to interpret this theme as creatively as possible and to work out the details as a structured project.

Between early October and mid-November of 1994, over twelve thousand entries displayed exceptional creativity, empathy, and originality in their ideas and wishes. Originally, KLM had decided to award ten first prizes, but the entries were so remarkable, they increased it to twelve selections.

An international jury, chaired by former Dutch prime minister Ruud Lubbers, selected the winners. KLM will provide the prizewinners with more than just free air travel. The company will also pay for all other expenses incurred by the prizewinners to make their cherished dreams come true. KLM has made a total of 2,000 air tickets available for the contests. In addition to the twelve first prizes, eighty-one contestants have been awarded second prizes. These prizewinners will receive a round-trip ticket to the destination of their project.

The twelve prize winning projects feature a great diversity of ideas. The route networks of KLM and its U.S. partner Northwest Airlines, which span the world, will bridge the gaps between cultures across the globe.

Here are some of the winners and their dream projects:

- A disabled American woman, Joni Eareckson Tada, will be traveling to Ghana with a team of twenty-five specialists and therapists, where they will present the Ghanaian Association for the Physically Disabled with the gift of 200 wheelchairs.

  In her letter to KLM, Tada said, "Because I've lived in a wheelchair as a quadriplegic for over 27 years, I'm aware of how a wheelchair is not something that 'confines,' but something that can set a person like me 'free.' But I'm the fortunate one. There are 540 million disabled people in the world and a need for over 18 million wheelchairs. In most developing nations, a wheelchair can cost a person his life's savings."

- An American woman, Judith Berger, will bring together twenty-five

Annes, each from a different country, in Amsterdam in the summer of 1995 in memory of the famous dutch girl, Anne Frank, whose diary of her last days on earth during World War II has electrified the world. Berger's letter entry was simple and moving: "What personifies the theme of belief in the goodness of all people more than the poignant words of a young girl named Anne Frank? It would be a tribute to her memory to invite 25 young girls from around the world, who also bear the name of 'Anne.' These girls would spend a week in Amsterdam, and each one would keep her own diary of the friendships she had made, and what she learned of the cultures of other countries. All the diaries would be published, with an official ceremony at the Anne Frank House. The collection of 'the diaries of Anne' could be sold worldwide, and proceeds would go to sponsor the similar trip each year."

- A man from the United States, Charles Watson, will be leading a project for the construction of a much needed clinic in the suburbs of Conakry, Guinea. He plans to complete the project in just seven days with the help of twenty-four professional workers from the United States and Europe.

- Thanks to the idea of a woman from the Netherlands, ten young shoe-shine boys from the fairy-tale city of Istanbul, Turkey, will be given a week's vacation at the wonderland theme park, "De Efteling," in the Netherlands.

- A Dutch cook working in Moscow will lead a cookery course in the Netherlands for a group of Russian volunteers who prepare meals for elderly people in Moscow. While the Russian cooks are away getting their training, KLM will cater the meals for the elderly Muscovites.

◆ ◆ ◆

Twenty companies have been named to a consumer's honor roll by the Council on Economic Priorities, based on eight major areas of social responsibility.

Consumer's Honor Roll — Companies with a Heart

The twenty companies, rated on the basis of corporate stewardship of the environment, opportunities for women and for minorities, workplace issues, family benefits, community outreach, charitable giving, and corporate disclosure are Adolph Coors, Anheuser-Busch, Aveda Corp., Avon Products, Ben & Jerry's, Colgate-Palmolive, Dayton Hudson, Digital Equipment, General Mills, Giant Food, Grand Metropolitan PLC, Hewlett-Packard, Johnson & Johnson, S.C. Johnson & Son, Kellogg Co., Levi Strauss & Co., Nordstrom Inc., Rhino Records, Tom's of Maine, and WarnerLambert.

The 20 "winners" and 171 other companies are rated on the above criteria in *Shopping for a Better World*, from Sierra Club Books.

CHAPTER 7

POSITIVE
POLITICIANS

Our political institutions work remarkably well. They are designed to
clang against each other. The noise
is democracy at work.

—Michael Novak

Watergate, Whitewater, Republicans,
Democrats, Liberals, Conservatives,
from the Great Society to the Contract
with America — these are all the stuff of
politics and politicians.

Polls place the public's trust in politicians somewhere near (sometimes
above and sometimes below) used car
salesmen . . . an all time low. But do they
all live off the fat of the lobbyists? Lie,
cheat, and steal? Compromise their eth-
ics while living from election to election
feeding off the public trough?

Aren't some of them dedicated public

servants, serving their constituencies with honor and ideals, in a positive way?

Yes. The "Positive Politicians" selected for this chapter came from all over the country. Some serve at the national level in the Senate or the House of Representatives. Some as governors, others as mayors. They all have a common link — they are honorable people who chose politics as a way to serve their communities, right wrongs, and improve lives.

Most of them don't receive an abundance of news coverage for this, nor do they seek it. These are people who are proud to serve.

Twenty-five years ago, when I was the publisher of *The Good News Paper*, I ran a weekly column titled "Positive Politicians." To prevent my readers from prejudging the men and women featured each week based on their party affiliation and labels of conservative or liberal, I did not include these labels when I wrote about them. I continue that policy in the stories that follow, in the hope that you will read about *who* they are, *what* they are doing, and *why* they are doing it, instead of what party they belong to, or what slant their views fall into. I hope in this way that you can objectively judge them for their positive actions unencumbered by political prejudice. For those of you who just *have* to know, their party affiliations are listed at the end of this chapter.

◆ ◆ ◆

The Reverend Doug Tanner is the executive director of The Faith in Politics Institute in Washington, D.C. The Institute is ecumenical and interreligious and is committed to strengthening participants to exercise effective, nonpartisan leadership on issues of major moral importance. Reverend Tanner supplies us with our first Positive Politician story.

Spiritual Politics in the Real World — Representative Glenn Poshard

Washington, D.C.

I met Glenn Poshard about a month after he had been elected to the Congress from southern Illinois in 1988. Glenn had been a high school American history teacher and an Illinois state senator. When he learned of my credentials as a "man of the cloth," Glenn shared some of his own religious identity: He was a Southern Baptist who read a lot of Thomas Merton and made regular pilgrimages to Gethsemane (the Trappist monastery near Louisville where Merton lived and wrote) for periods of silent retreat. That combination caught my attention.

One Sunday night several months later, Glenn called me at home, and asked if we could have dinner some night that week.

The following evening we took a table at an Italian restaurant on Pennsylvania Avenue, and Glenn shared some of his soul. Some of what he was feeling was typical freshman loneliness, exacerbated by the fact that his wife, Jo, had remained in Illinois to teach school. (This is a common pattern in Congress, particularly among younger members and their spouses.) At a deeper level, though, Glenn was yearning for distinctly spiritual companionship. He had begun to feel the pull of political pressures in ways he didn't like, and he wondered where it might take him. He didn't have anyone in Washington with whom he felt free enough to air the anxiety and to sort things out. I told

Glenn I would be willing to try to play that role for him.

We got together a couple more times, just the two of us. Then I asked Glenn if he'd like for me to seek out one or two other people who were both experienced in politics and consciously seeking their own spiritual growth; we could form a small group to meet regularly for mutual discernment and encouragement and for reflection on life in politics.

When Glenn said yes, I recruited White House staffer Anne Bartley, who chairs the board of The Faith of Politics Institute, and Joe Eldridge, a fellow clergyman who works as a human rights advocate. We began to meet from 7:30 to 9:00 on Wednesday mornings in Glenn's office.

By October of 1989, the four of us had developed enough trust to begin to taste the fruits of our covenant. It was then that Glenn shared the spiritual and ethical dilemma that gave rise to the real drama of our life together.

"I need you guys to help me with something. I'm supposed to be raising money for my re-election campaign, and I just don't want to do it. One of my colleagues has told me that my goal as a freshman congressman should be to raise $1,000 a day. You know, I did it the first time like everybody said to do. I raised $430,000 — almost $25,000 of it from PACs. (Political action committees.) And I just hate the thought of doing it again." "My district is almost 20 percent unemployed," Glenn said.

Shutdowns of southern Illinois coal mines had given Glenn's Congressional district the highest unemployment of any rural district in the country. "I can't ask my people for that kind of money. If I have to raise money, I'd a lot rather do it for a project back home to buy jackets and shoes for school kids who don't have them than to pay it to media consultants and stations. I can raise campaign money from the PACs, but I've already become uncomfortable with it. I feel like I have to commit myself before I've had a chance to study their issues at all thoroughly, so I don't really know where I come out in my own heart and mind. And I don't want to scare off an opponent; I think my people deserve a choice."

Anne, Joe, and I looked at each other in amazement. Are you serious? We know fund-raising can be a pain, but what do you mean you don't want to scare off an opponent? You're not going to take full advantage of being an incumbent? You sound like Mr. Smith comes to Washington. We really like you, but you must be naive . . . unrealistic . . . some kind of a Pollyanna.

At the same time, as we watched Glenn's expression, there was an incredibly compelling charisma about him when he talked about campaigning on a minimal budget. By contrast, when he talked about having to go out and raise half a million dollars, he looked like a wet dish rag.

At the end of the meeting, none of the rest of us were convinced that Glenn would be likely to win with such an unconventional minimal budget approach. We were clear, though, that any capacities we had to discern the leading of the Spirit in Glenn Poshard's life told us he should follow his energy. The energy was in doing it differently — radically differently from conventional campaign wisdom. So we told Glenn, "This seems politically crazy to us, but you need to do it and we're with you."

The test came soon enough. After the 1990 census, politicians in Illinois had to face the loss of two congressional seats due to redistricting. Glenn Poshard's district had been carved into three pieces. Not one of the three new districts consisting of Glenn's former territory exceeded 40 percent.

In the one new district where Glenn had the strongest base, he would have to run against another more senior incumbent, Terry Bruce. An article in *Roll Call*, the Capitol Hill newspaper, compared campaign treasuries of all incumbents who were facing potential primary contests against other incumbents: Bruce had the most money of all, and Poshard had the least; the respective figures were $650,000 for Bruce and $20,000 for Glenn Poshard. The Primary date was March 17, 1992.

When the group last met before the Thanksgiving recess, Glenn was distraught and close to despair. He felt betrayed by his colleagues, some of whose prospects for re-election appeared to have been enhanced at Glenn's expense; he believed they could have more effectively fought for a redistricting plan that would give everyone a decent chance. Forswearing PAC donations and maximum contributions from individuals left a bitter aftertaste as he viewed the funding advantage of his opponent.

Hurt and anger led to thoughts of political vengeance. Anne, Joe, and I sadly explored with Glenn his options for the future. Some of them looked more attractive than a March Primary race against Bruce.

Glenn returned to Illinois, where he continued to search his soul. Did he have a chance? Could people be inspired to work for him against such odds? Glenn knew he had a message: It was about integrity and politics, and he had a hunch it might really resonate. But could he deliver it well enough in such a short time without an expensive media campaign?

He decided he could live with himself better if he tried and failed than if he didn't try. In December, Glenn announced that he would challenge Terry Bruce in the March primary.

The *Southern Illinoisan*, one of the district's major newspapers, editorialized: "Poshard is the only politician in Illinois with the courage and faith in his convictions, and in the electorate, to put them to the test."

When the votes were counted in Illinois' new 19th Congressional District on March 17, Glenn's convictions and the electorate he trusted had more than passed the test.

Glenn had defeated Terry Bruce by 62 percent to 38 percent. He had spent a total of $146,608 to Bruce's $704,015. None of his money had come from PACs, and no individual had contributed over $500. Glenn's 23-year-old son, Dennis, had managed the campaign. There were three paid campaign workers, none of whom was a professional.

His opponent had not only spent over $704,000, he had employed some of the best consultants in the business. He had done everything that candidates raise campaign money to do — except win.

Glenn Poshard had made up for his lack of a heavy mass media communications budget by a lot of hard work and old-fashioned organizing. He had sat down with key community and party leaders and discussed personal histories and shared values long enough for them to come to trust him. They then actively worked to bring the support of all their constituents who trusted them.

Glenn had interacted naturally and genuinely with people, whether he had spent several hours with them or two minutes. He believed in the fundamental good sense and fairness of the voters. That faith came through in personal conversations, in his public speeches, and in his simply produced ads that were cut late at night in a local studio. The contagion of the Poshard campaign was clear when 1,700 people turned out for a $10-a-person fund-raiser . . . yes, a $10-a-person fund raiser.

The week after the election, Glenn and I sat down in his office. We spent a couple of hours savoring the success of his faith in his convictions and in the electorate. As we recounted and reflected, I asked Glenn which issues and factors he thought had been the determining factors.

"The issues," Glenn stated with quiet confidence, "had to do with the broader state of the union in regard to representation and trust. My campaign refused to pull punches with people. We connected them with the reality of the whole, rather than the parochial. Terry ran an ad against me saying I had voted to cut Medicare in the 1990 Budget

Agreement. I responded, 'Yes, I voted to cut it as an alternative to eventually losing the entire Medicare system.' I defended the 5-cent gas tax in that vote as a way to pay for the improvements we need in bridges and highways now, instead of saddling our children with the debt. We showed people the bigger picture on every issue; we connected them with the bigger whole," he said.

"The campaign was one of integrity because we told the hard truth. People intuitively knew what it meant for the long haul. We in Congress generally don't trust people's judgments with the bigger picture. Instead, we wrap ourselves in security blankets. The system has kept the lid on, but people are beginning to make the connection. The pot is about to boil over. If the Congress is going to help save the country, it has to stop worrying about saving itself."

"Glenn, where did you find the clarity and the courage — to begin to do it differently from most of your colleagues?" I asked.

"A lot of it came from the group," Glenn answered, referring to our regular gathering. "The time with you guys has been critical. You were the ones with whom I felt enough trust to talk about the fund-raising issue and to make that decision. I don't think I would have stayed with it without you. There were a lot of times I was tempted to change my mind. If there hadn't been anyone to whom I held myself accountable on it, I probably would have.

"Everyone in Washington encourages you to vote 'safely' for political reasons. All the time I hear, 'Your first job is to get back here . . . to get re-elected.' No one asks, Where is your gut? Where is your heart? Where is your soul?

"The group is the place that pulls me forward. I can go to my family for comfort, but not for that. You guys strengthen my capacity to listen to the inner voice. You give me the encouragement I need to follow through. No one else around here holds me accountable to the truths I know most deeply.

"One of those is that there's nothing creative about acting vindictively. In the final days of the redistricting process, when I learned about the map and I felt so betrayed, my first reactions were anger and vindictiveness. The group anchored my dealing with that until I had put it in perspective.

"When I finally decided to run, I saw it as a chance worth taking. By then I wasn't doing it out of blind vengeance. I think I would have lost if that had been the case. I wouldn't have been able to focus on the whole, to educate the constituency, if I had gone in angry. All that involved some heavy soul searching.

"When I made the decision, there was a profoundly positive spiritual experience of abandoning my own self in it. Ultimately, every time you have the courage to believe in that, you become a vessel for something greater, and you bring people along."

—By Reverend Doug Tanner
  Doug Tanner is executive director of The Faith and Politics Institute in Washington, D.C.

◆ ◆ ◆

Two of the negative stereotypes that persist in the public's mind is that politicians are a bunch of old men who don't keep their campaign promises. Fidel Vargas is twenty-six, he kept his campaign promises, and he is still there.

Fidel Vargas — California's Youngest Mayor

Baldwin Park, California

In 1992 a security guard refused to let him walk into a U.S. Conference of Mayors meeting in Washington. Not unreasonable, considering that Fidel Vargas, as California's youngest mayor, could have easily passed for a courier. Since he receives only three thousand dollars a year for running city hall in Baldwin Park (population, seventy-two thousand), Vargas can probably lay claim to providing taxpayers with the best value of any politician in the country. Elected at age twenty-three and reelected by a large majority in 1993, Vargas promised to combat prostitution and drug dealing, and kept his promise. He stepped up police patrols and prohibited motels from renting rooms more than once in twenty-four hours. As a result, arrests fell from 150 to 5.

It wasn't conventional activism that propelled this young man into politics. It was graffiti. He saw a wall covered with it, and was bothered. "I went to a few city council members and they were really nonchalant about it. 'Well . . . we're doing the best we can.' Next, he went to his friends and asked them to run for office. No one would. So Vargas did — and won. In his term of office, property values have risen and tax receipts are up. And he still hates graffiti: "Graffiti sends a really bad message to the community: that the community doesn't really care enough to have a clean, safe environment for their kids to grow up in."

Among reforms Vargas cites during his tenure: a new bike patrol for the city's police, holding town meetings at a local elementary school instead of city hall ("it's a less intimidating atmosphere"), and a new youth advisory board that has a voice on the city council and helps develop programs for young people.

Vargas is also a proponent of "midnight basketball," the much-praised program that became the target of Republican ridicule during the crime bill fight in Congress last summer.

Vargas doesn't buy the idea that there's a gap between politics and service. "Politics," he says, "is community service. Local politics in your local city, that is public service." But he, too, encounters the disdain for politics that has penetrated most communities over the past thirty years. "I don't call myself a politician," says the young mayor. "I call myself an elected official, but we need to focus on how to change that perception on the local level. When people get upset, they go to the city council, they don't go to Congress."

And what does this Harvard graduate have to say about fellow members of the "twenty-something" generation? "We're forced to grow up with drugs, AIDS, and poverty. Knowing that it is impossible to buy a home you're forced to grow up fast. If anything, we are responsible and wise and dependable, not the flakes that we are perceived to be." Fidel Vargas is on the right track to reach his goal of a seat in the United States Senate.

◆ ◆ ◆

Like Fidel Vargas, Bret Schundler, thirty-five, was not a likely prospect to be the mayor of his city.

Bret Schundler —
An Unexpected Choice

He is the last person one would expect to see running Jersey City, New Jersey. More than 50 percent of the population is nonwhite, over 14 percent of the city's residents are on welfare, and his opponent's party has controlled City Hall since 1917.

Bret Schundler is white, prosperous (he once sold bonds on Wall Street), and a fair-haired boy of his party. What makes him stand out as mayor of Jersey City, however, is his accomplishments since being elected in 1992.

In a mayor's office that was so corrupt that the desk of one of his predecessors was actually rigged to drop bribes into visitors' laps, Schundler's fiscal proposals present a national model for urban reform — while casting the young mayor as a potential candidate for national office. Schundler preaches a gospel of lower taxes, less government, and "voucherizing" city services so that people decide for themselves who sweeps their streets and educates their kids. Says the mayor: "We want those directly affected by services to be in charge of hiring them." And, today, the only thing that desk drops into visitor's laps is an opportunity to make their city better.

He started out his career as a journalist. An observer of problems can only do so much, however. That's why Henry Bonilla jumped into politics.

Henry Bonilla — From the Barrios to Congress

As a local television reporter, Henry Bonilla moved around the barrios of South Texas with an ease that gave him an edge on the competition. His understanding of a community that includes some of the poorest people in the nation, however, eventually inspired him to do more than report about other people's pain.

Bonilla, forty, plunged into Texas politics in 1992 with the aggression of a linebacker and sacked his four-term incumbent to become the first Hispanic congressman from Texas for his party. When he arrived in Washington, D.C., from San Antonio, he was assigned to the House Appropriations Committee, a position not held by a freshman from his party for twenty-five years.

"You can have anything you ask for, if

you are willing to step forward and work," is how Bonilla sees it. "His future is open-ended," says Speaker of the House Newt Gingrich. "He's tremendously intelligent, very, very competent, very organized." And a positive voice for his South Texas constituents who believe in his work ethic and his honesty.

◆ ◆ ◆

Cynthia McKinney, thirty-nine, didn't fit the mold of traditional politicians when she threw her hat in the ring. She was African-American, she was from a southern state, and she was a single parent. That didn't keep her out of the race though . . . far from it.

Cynthia McKinney — She Didn't Fit the Mold

Cynthia McKinney may be the only elected official in the country to show up for work in gold lamé sneakers. As her choice of footwear might indicate, she is not one of the more timid members of Congress.

"Whenever you see a good fight, get in it," is how this woman describes her leadership philosophy. Elected Georgia's first African-American congresswoman in 1992, McKinney, a single parent, has been battling every day to improve the lives of the poor. She successfully fought for a larger tax break for working families and also for an EPA investigation into environmental contamination of an impoverished Georgia community.

In addition, she has backed legislation to fund breast cancer research and to protect access to abortion clinics. "Nobody minds when I lobby them because they always get a hug and a kiss," says the self-described maverick congresswoman. "I don't practice the same good-ol'-boy, business-as-usual politics."

(Editor's note: Fidel Vargas, Henry Bonilla, Bret Schundler, and Cynthia McKinney were among the fifty chosen by *Time* magazine in 1994 as our future top leaders.)

◆ ◆ ◆

Our final selection for Positive Politicians is retired now, but this former congresswoman's influence is still felt on

Capitol Hill by members of both parties — the influence of her service, compassion, and kindness. Craig Wilson of USA Today *wrote this feature story about her.*

Lindy Boggs — A Southern Gentlewoman

Lindy Boggs and Vice-President Al Gore go back a long way. A very long way. Way back to the days when Boggs used to bounce the future V.P. on her knee.

In November 1994, at a party to celebrate Boggs's just-published memoir, *Washington Through a Purple Veil: Memoirs of a Southern Woman* (Harcourt Brace, $24.95), Gore came to pay homage to the woman who has known 11 presidents and every mover and shaker on Capitol Hill for the last 50 years.

A rarity in politics, former congresswoman Boggs is adored, almost to the point of veneration. No one at the party could recall anyone who didn't like her. "You not only will not find that person, no such person exists anywhere on earth," said Gore, putting to rest any rumor that a Lindy Boggs enemy might be lurking out there somewhere. "She is a truly unique and wonderful woman."

This is all a bit hyperbolic, of course, but Boggs, ever the Southern lady, has made a career out of getting along, smoothing ruffled feathers on the biggest birds on the hill.

"She has a wonderful ability to treat everyone with dignity," says longtime friend and Boggs family attorney Robert Barnett. "She was never disagreeable even in disagreement. It's not her style. That's why people loved her."

At breakfast the next morning, Boggs, now 78, is gracious about the accolades. But her way of doing business is second nature to her. She says her decades of service were rooted in her childhood.

"Growing up in the South, I think there's a feeling of noblesse oblige. You have an obligation to serve," says Boggs, who was raised in rather privileged surroundings in the plantation parishes of Louisiana. She hails from an old family — 15 bridesmaids at her wedding. You get the picture.

While it all seems to be a charmed life on the surface, Boggs' tale comes with its share of tragedies: She lost a son shortly after birth; daughter Barbara, who was mayor of Princeton, N.J., died of cancer in 1990; and her husband, Hale, the House majority speaker and a star in the Democratic party, disappeared in a plane crash in Alaska in 1972. Boggs took over his seat after his death, serving in the House from 1973 to 1990.

She says she was ahead of the game because she already knew the cast of characters through her years as a congressman's wife. And with her propensity to act as a "go-between," she was able to push through bills ranging from civil rights to equal pay for women.

The late Rep. Bill Nichols of Alabama gave her the ultimate compliment years ago, saying, "Lindy's just one of the boys."

Rep. Barney Frank, D-Mass., who worked with Boggs on the hill, says she got so much done because "People knew how genuine she is. You couldn't fake it for that long. They respected her sincerity."

But isn't there *anyone* who doesn't like her?

"Newt Gingrich," says Frank.

Boggs does make one reference to Gingrich in her book, saying that she was surprised he climbed to the position of

GOP whip, adding a quote from a GOP insider admitting they needed someone "mean" if they were ever to regain control of the House. But, as is her style, she quickly put a good spin on the Speaker of the House. "For the good of the nation and of the House, I know he will mellow."

Those who worked with her on the book tell how she would relate juicy Capitol Hill tales of yore, only to say "but we're not putting *that* in the book."

"She really does have a nice thing to say about everybody," says her editor Claire Wachtel.

Boggs says she wrote the book because she had one simple message: "That despite all the warts on the body of the government of the United States of America, it is still the strongest, the most compatible to a better human condition and the strongest defender of liberties."

The 1994 National American Mother of the Year, Lindy Boggs is now a grandmother of eight and a great-grandmother of three, and she still likes to talk about doing the right thing.

She remains convinced that public office is a public trust, an honorable profession. She stresses that over and over in her book. And those who know Lindy know better than to argue that point.

—By Craig T. Wilson
Copyright 1994, *USA Today.*
Reprinted with permission.

I promised at the beginning of this chapter to reveal the party affiliations, and here they are: Poshard (D), Vargas (D), Schundler (R), Bonilla (R), McKinney (D), Boggs (D).

CHAPTER 8

HIGH TECH — HIGH HOPES FOR THE FUTURE

Discovery consists of looking at the same thing as everyone else and thinking something different.

—Roger von Oech

I am not technologically proficient. But I love gadgets. I'm a mechanical idiot, but I am awed by all the wonderful little gizmos that make my life so easy. I'm old enough to remember when cars didn't have power steering, automatic transmissions, or even power brakes, let alone power antilock brakes. When my wife and I were married over thirty-four years ago, we even had to defrost our refrigerator . . . automatic defrost hadn't been invented.

The one-room school I attended out in the country had a crank telephone —

three cranks got you a cranky operator (just kidding, Ma Bell), who would make your call for you. Our family didn't even get a phone until 1950, and then it was a nine-party line. Our first black and white television set arrived in 1955, along with "snowy" pictures and a cathode tube that stuck out three feet from the back of it. Progress. Today, virtually every household in America has automobiles that have computers in them to keep them running at maximum efficiency, engines that don't need tuneups for the first forty to fifty thousand miles, and safety equipment fit for the first man in space.

Touch-dialing telephones of all sizes and shapes with sound traveling by satellites in space and fiberoptic telephone wires that deliver our voices with such clarity an opera singer could break a glass if she sang over them.

Television brings us full-color images instantaneously from any part of the world, with stereo sound optional. Speaking of sound, scratchy 78-rpm records have been replaced with compact digital discs that reproduce sound so accurately you feel you're in the orchestra pit.

And computers. Ah, yes, computers. The world today is run by computers, no doubt about it. The majority of advances in science, medicine, industry, entertainment, publishing, and virtually everything else are owed to computers.

Just twenty-five years ago the computer I am using to write this book would have taken up a whole floor. Today it fits on a three-by-four-foot desk with room to spare. And engineers who used to have to carry slide rules with them to compute their complex formulas, which often took weeks or months to complete, now can do them on a laptop computer while traveling six hundred miles per hour in a jumbo jet, and complete the equations in seconds or minutes.

The list could go on and on, but this chapter is about just a few of the Good News stories that have come out in the last twelve months about high-tech developments you can already use or will be able to in the near future. Medical technology dominates this first edition of *America's Good News Almanac* by this editor's choice — but breakthroughs in every area are happening so rapidly that by the time you read these stories, there will undoubtedly be hundreds of new developments in the fast-growing world of high technology.

◆ ◆ ◆

Just weeks before Stephen and Tammy's first son was due to be born, doctors discovered a life-threatening cyst on the unborn infant's lung. They had only one way to save his life. Operate. But it had never been done before.

Doctors Save Baby's Life — Before He's Born!

Shreveport, Louisiana

Little Sam Nichols celebrated a very special first Christmas last year. He is the first baby ever to undergo treatment for a life-threatening lung cyst while still in his mother's womb.

Doctor's discovered the deadly condition on Christmas Eve in 1993, just eight weeks before Sam was born. Determined to save the unborn infant's life, specialists inserted a needle into the cyst and drained it — not once, but six times! Then, less than twenty-four hours after he was born, the tiny baby underwent delicate surgery to remove the cyst.

Incredibly, Sam is now perfectly healthy as he enters his second year of life — and his ecstatic parents call him their "miracle child." "I am absolutely sure Sam would have died had we not drained the cyst," said Dr. Mark Brown, of Louisiana State University Medical Center in Shreveport, Louisiana, where the operation was performed.

The boy's mother, Tammy, twenty-three, gushed: "My husband Stephen and I have two daughters we love dearly, but Sam is something special. He's the happiest baby I ever saw. It's as if he somehow knows how close he came to dying and appreciates every moment he's alive. He's my miracle baby!"

Sam's dramatic ordeal began when an ultrasound test revealed a huge cyst in his lung that was causing heart failure. "The doctors told us the cyst was preventing Sam's heart from pumping blood. It was also stopping his lungs from developing," said Tammy, an administrative assistant from Springhill, Louisiana. "Unless quick action was taken, Sam most likely would die."

That's when doctors at State University Medical Center in Shreveport proposed a revolutionary procedure. For the first time ever in medical history, they would surgically drain the cyst while Sam was still in his mother's womb.

Although it meant she might go into premature labor, Tammy agreed to the treatment. On December 27, 1993, Tammy was given local anesthesia and a needle was inserted through her abdominal wall into her womb.

The needle penetrated Sam's chest, went into the cyst, and drained the fluid. Doctors performed the twenty-minute procedure five more times. Finally, on February 16, 1994, Sam Nichols was born.

"When I saw my five-pound-eleven-ounce son for the first time, I was overjoyed!" said Tammy. "But I knew he wasn't out of the woods yet. The next day doctors decided to remove the cyst. The two-hour surgery was a complete success. Sam went home a week later — and today he's doing great!"

"Sam is a wonderful, healthy child with a completely normal life ahead of him," said Dr. Brown, assistant professor of pediatric surgery at Louisiana State University.

More than 1.5 million Americans break some kind of a bone in their body every year. Recovery is often slow, and always accompanied by that ugly old cast . . . but something new that could change all that is now in clinical trials.

Geologist's Invention May Help Set Broken Bones

Cupertino, California

A remarkable new "bone paste" that can be injected directly into broken bones, where it hardens in ten minutes, could dramatically improve treatment for the more than 1.5 million Americans who break bones every year.

For many patients, including the 300,000 who suffer a broken hip each year, the new material could mean less pain after surgery and far shorter hospital stays, which in turn could translate into millions of dollars in health care savings.

The new material, called Norian SRS and described by its inventors in the March 24, 1995, issue of the journal *Science*, becomes as strong as real bone about twelve hours after injection.

Because it is virtually identical to natural bone in its mineral composition, the substance is subject to the same perpetual process of resorption and repair all bone undergoes. That means it is molded by the body into the correct shape and is replaced within months by new, real bone.

And, because the new material is bio-compatible, it does not trigger an immune response, as usually happens with foreign substances, which would cause the body to reject it.

"It's a new technology that enables orthopedic surgeons to do things they just haven't been able to do before. There's just nothing like it," said Dr. Brent Constantz, who says he got the idea for the paste in 1985 while studying coral at the University of California, Santa Cruz.

The material, now in clinical trials at twelve centers nationwide, can be used to hold together splintered bones, to fill gaps in bones caused by osteoporosis, and to reinforce the metal plates and screws used for severely broken hips and other bones.

The bone paste has been tested successfully in a handful of patients with wrist fractures at Massachusetts General Hospital, as well as in clinical trials for hip, knee, shoulder, and wrist fractures in Sweden and the Netherlands.

Norian SRS bone paste, which has not yet been approved by the Food and Drug Administration, is the brainchild of Brent R. Constantz, a geologist who specializes in crystallography. He is the chief executive of Norian Corp. of Cupertino, California.

◆ ◆ ◆

Cancer researchers have known for years that cancer cells have the ability to grow and expand almost forever, unlike healthy cells that age and eventually die as they divide. They didn't know why until now . . . and their recent discovery has monumental possibilities.

Enzyme May Halt Cancer and Aging

Menlo Park, California

In a finding that opens the door to the development of less toxic, more effective anticancer drugs, and perhaps even to new drugs to prevent aging, researchers at a northern California company have discovered that virtually all human tumors contain an enzyme that blocks the biological clocks of tumor cells, allowing them to grow and proliferate virtually forever.

Normal cells, which do not contain the enzyme, lose a little bit of their DNA every time they divide, weakening them and eventually forcing replication to grind to a halt.

But in the presence of the newly discovered enzyme, called telomerase, the DNA of tumor cells is refreshed and renewed with every division, liberating them from the normal aging process.

The occurrence of the enzyme in ovarian cancer cells was reported earlier this year, but that report met with some skepticism, according to molecular biologist Al Rabson, of the National Cancer Institute. Now a team at Geron Corp., in Menlo Park, reported in the journal *Science* what Rabson calls "much more impressive evidence" that telomerase is present in virtually every human tumor studied.

The company already has identified several chemicals that block the action of telomerase and hopes to begin testing them in humans within two years.

The advantage of this approach, researchers said, is that most human cells do not contain the enzyme and thus would be immune to any effects of the inhibitors. Furthermore, because the unusual enzyme seems to be present in nearly all tumors, any agent that could incapacitate the enzyme would work, theoretically, in all types of cancer.

"This has got the properties you'd be looking for in a magic bullet," said Huber Warner, a molecular biologist for the National Institute on Aging.

Conversely, if researchers could induce healthy cells to begin manufacturing the enzyme, it might retard the aging process, particularly in highly vulnerable cells such as those in the brain.

"This is certainly a finding that will stimulate a great deal of interest in researchers studying the basic biology of aging, as well as cancer," said gerontologist Richard Hodes, director of the National Institute on Aging. "Long-term, our best hope for [halting aging] will depend on a better understanding of the biology of these systems."

Scientists have long known that mammalian cells, unlike those of microorganisms, have a finite lifetime. When researchers attempt to grow them in the lab, the cells replicate about sixty times before they mysteriously die out.

Studies by a variery of researchers, especially biologist Elizabeth H. Blackburn, of the University of California, Berkeley, showed that the key to immortality in microorganisms is a long fragment of DNA, called a telomere, that sits on the end of each cell's chromosomes like the tip of a shoelace. Chromosomes are packets of DNA that contain the blueprint for reproducing an organism, and researchers now believe that telomeres keep the DNA stable, just as the tip keeps the shoelace from fraying.

The telomere represents a kind of bookkeeping device that controls aging. Each time a cell replicates, a fragment of the telomere is broken off and lost. When the whole telomere is gone, the chromosome breaks down and the cell dies. Microorganisms were found to have an enzyme — telomerase — that replaces the broken-off fragments, allowing the cells to continue thriving forever.

In the new study, researchers at Geron and the University of Texas Southwestern Medical Center in Dallas used a new, highly sensitive test to show that telomerase was present in 98 of 100 human tumor cell lines grown in the laboratory and in 90 of 101 tissue samples from twelve types of human tumors.

Geron scientists are now isolating chemicals that block the action of telomerase. Such drugs would halt the growth of tumor cells and make them more susceptible to attack by conventional chemotherapy.

◆ ◆ ◆

A baby in a hospital without its mother has a hard time sleeping. Drug-addicted babies have a particularly hard time. A former rock 'n' roll record producer may seem like an unlikely inventor of a device that solves the problem, but Terry Woodford finally had an audience he could put to sleep!

A Heartfelt Baby Lullaby

Colorado Springs, Colorado

The babies in Penrose Community Hospital in Colorado Springs pediatric unit were, well, sleeping like babies.

Babies do indeed sleep a lot. But, like adults, the strange environment of a hospital makes it tough for babies to get a restful sleep. So nurses here found a way to sooth their tiny charges without drugs.

A recording of children's songs accompanied by the sound of a human heart puts them to sleep or quiets them almost instantly, said Jan DeBruin, the hospital's clinical manager for pediatrics.

"The response is so quick it's hard to believe," she said.

Down the hall, a 9-month-old girl with Down's syndrome who was crying because she couldn't have a drink of water instantly fell silent when DeBruin switched on the tape player.

Nurses also use the tapes for young patients who are frightened by such things as needles, surgery or being fitted with an intravenous feeding tube.

"It relieves the anxiety for the children and even seems to work pretty good on our nurses and the parents," DeBruin said.

The soothing music is especially helpful with crack babies or drug-addicted infants going through withdrawal, said

Marcie Tourville, a Penrose Community nurse.

The "Baby-Go-to-Sleep" tapes, made by a Colorado Springs company, a tape player and special speakers that fit under or inside a foam mattress are provided free to hospitals and child care agencies nationwide by J.C. Penney and the inventor, former rock 'n' roll record producer Terry Woodford.

Unlike other lullaby tapes, Woodford's has the pervasive sound of a real heartbeat and the engineering to match the tunes to that rhythm, he said.

"When mothers rock their babies, they hold them against their chests, close to the heart," he said.

Woodford, who wrote, recorded and produced six gold records and worked with the Temptations, the Supremes, Barbara Mandrell and Hank Williams Jr., said coming up with something to put children to sleep was the biggest challenge of his career.

"When you make music for money, your goal is to evoke an emotion. You try to excite people so they will go out and buy your records," he said. "Putting them to sleep isn't something you want to do."

But Woodford was intrigued by the challenge, as well as the potential marketability.

His first effort was a holiday tape that he gave to friends and several day care centers. It wasn't a big success, but some reported it did get their children to sleep, he said.

That launched a 9-year research and development quest that evolved into a new career, he said.

He visited hospital nurseries and neonatal units to measure sound levels and talked to doctors and nurses about using sound in their care of children.

"Being in a neonatal unit is like being a prisoner of war. You are confined to a small box, strapped with tubes, naked under bright lights, poked and prodded several times an hour, and subjected to startling noises like buzzers and monitor alarms," Woodford said.

Crying increases the stress on a seriously ill baby and burns calories it needs to heal and grow, the nurses told Woodford.

They shared their expertise in health care and he shared his knowledge of music and its effect on people.

Woodford needed calming music — he

wanted to capture compassion.

"I had to go through several singers before I found the one who could convey that."

He found Cindy Wheeler, a former Colorado College student and local entertainer who moved on to a music career in Nashville.

First he recorded a human heartbeat and then experimented with overlaying different children's tunes.

"I didn't know that hearts didn't beat in tempo. When I found out, the thing became a personal challenge to find tunes that could match that rhythm. I spent a year experimenting and recording until I got five lullabies I was happy with."

Classical music and new age tunes won't work, he said.

"They are too complex, dynamic and unstructured."

Children's nursery rhymes such as "Mary Had a Little Lamb," "Row, Row, Row Your Boat" or "Rockabye Baby" are simple, repetitious, and harmonious, Woodford said. Nurses who tried the tapes were eager for more, he said.

Woodford struck a deal with J.C. Penney after their nationwide infant wear buyer tried a tape on her insomniac 2-year-old. More than 5,000 hospitals and special care centers across the country have received the equipment for their neonatal, nursery and pediatric units.

Then Woodford began looking for other ways to use the tape in medicine. Nurses working with Alzheimer's patients wanted something as an alternative to drug treatment for those who sometimes become violent.

What he thought would be soothing — romantic adult tunes such as "Moon River" and "Amazing Grace" — appeared to agitate, rather than calm patients.

He said that was probably because the songs stirred strong memories and emotions. Children's tunes apparently make the elderly feel safe and secure, so nurses use the baby tape.

Woodford sold his rock music business and now devotes his time to his new company, Audio-Therapy Innovations, which he moved to Colorado Springs about three years ago.

"I guess when I look back, I made a few marks on the world as a record producer and songwriter, but I don't think any of them exactly made the world a better place," Woodford said. "This, I think, does."

—By Dru Wilson
December 27, 1994. Reprinted with permission of the *Colorado Springs Gazette Telegraph.*

◆ ◆ ◆

Within the next two years, scientists will start human studies on a breakthrough gene therapy program that may revolutionize the treatment of heart problems.

Designer Genes for Your Heart

Dallas, Texas

Scientists are aggressively exploring ways to treat blocked arteries, high cholesterol, and a host of heart problems with designer genes, experts reported in late 1994.

"We've really moved into a new era of gene therapy," says Dr. Jeffrey Leiden, of the University of Chicago School of Medicine.

Rapid progress in animal studies had advanced gene therapy from the simple idea of replacing a missing gene to designing genes to intervene in a host of complex diseases.

New approaches presented in Dallas at the 1994 American Heart Association meeting included:

- "Bio-bypass surgery," in which genes are implanted on the heart to induce new blood vessels to grow around blocked arteries, reported by Dr. Ron Crystal, New York Hospital/Cornell Medical Center.
- Implanting genes in arteries treated with balloon angioplasty to prevent the artery from reclosing. In about 40 percent of angioplasty cases, artery wall cells injured during the procedure respond by growing out of control like a tumor. Animal studies show the unregulated cell growth can be interrupted; the approach may one day even be applied to cancer.
- Implanting a gene that makes red blood cells into muscle cells, then using the cells as red blood cell factories. The approach is designed for people with severe anemia, such as those with kidney failure.

- Implanting genes directly on the heart area damaged by heart attack to grow new muscle, reported by Lawrence Kedes, University of Southern California, Los Angeles.
- Sending genes to the liver to treat cholesterol disorders, reported by Dr. James Wilson, University of Pennsylvania. In animal studies, scientists can design just about any cholesterol level they want.

Human studies on these therapies are expected within two years.

◆ ◆ ◆

For people who have lost arms or legs, the advancements in artificial limbs have been marvelous. From cumbersome hooks for hands, and rigid, immobile artificial legs, the world of prosthetics has advanced to devices with very near the abilities of the original limb. But there has always been one very important thing missing — the sense of touch. Until 1995.

A "Reach Out and Touch" Bionic Limb

When Chuck Tiemann lost his right leg and left arm in an accident fifteen years ago, he thought many of life's simple joys were forever lost to him.

Now the thirty-nine-year-old Braman, Oklahoma, man had regained some of those lost sensations as part of the first group of amputees to test a new generation of artificial limbs that return the sense of touch.

"The first time I could reach out and touch my wife's hand and feel the warmth after more than a decade — that was a very emotional moment," he said.

The sensory system is being developed by the Sabolich Prosthetic Research Center in Oklahoma City, a division of NovaCare Inc., a large physical rehabilitation company based in King of Prussia, Pennsylvania.

The system uses pressure and temperature sensors and electronic circuits embedded in false arms and legs. These circuits are connected to electrodes inside a prosthesis socket that touch the skin of the truncated limb.

The electrodes transfer pressure

pulses, or sensations of heat or cold, to surviving nerve endings.

John Sabolich, NovaCare's national prosthetics director, said two years of tests began in the spring of 1995, and will eventually involve 120 amputees nationwide. The National Institutes of Health has contributed about five hundred thousand dollars toward the research. The products could be on the market in under a year.

Researchers have been testing these sensory systems on one or two people at a time in the 1950s, said Clayton Van Doren, a professor who does such work at Case Western Reserve University in Cleveland. But he said Sabolich's work is the first commercial application.

"The single thing we most need right now is exactly what Sabolich is doing — putting something on the market."

Patients have described the sense of touch they get as a tingling, "like the feeling you get when your foot's asleep," Sabolich said.

Tiemann, a former utility lineman who lost his leg and arm in an accident atop an electrical pole, said he likes feeling the clutch of his pickup truck, or knowing the temperature of a cup of coffee he's about to grab with his prosthetic hand.

He said the sensory systems let amputees regain a sense of normalcy. "When I woke up from my amputations, I felt mutilated," Tiemann recalled. Tiemann wondered if he could ever live a regular life again. Fifteen years later, the answer is, "Yes, I can, without a doubt."

◆ ◆ ◆

A great new 'zine was launched in March 1995 that features the latest information on new technology in clear, simple language and without the hype. It's appropriately titled:

What Next?!

New York, New York

Some of the new products and future technological developments discussed in the first issue of *What Next?!* were the following:

- People with allergies may have to wait about seven years, but help is on the way. According to the publication, researchers are working to technologically eliminate allergies such as hay fever and asthma. Companies including Genentech and Tanox Biosystems have designed a molecule that locks onto troublesome antibodies, those responsible for triggering allergic responses, and clinical trials of related drugs are underway.

- In another two or three years, *What Next?!* says, doctors will routinely be using specific proteins to repair broken bones.
- Within the next couple of years plastics may be so biodegradable, they'll be edible. Scientists at the Center for Crop Utilization Research at Iowa State University have developed plastics made from the starch and proteins in soybeans and corn. Even if we don't eat it, we can use the plastics and they can be ground up for cattle feed.
- Available in 1995 is the GloveTalker, a portable communications system designed for people who have lost the ability to speak through illness or accident and do not have sufficient use of their hands for American Sign Language. It translates

small hand or finger movements into audible phrases. (Greenleaf Medical Systems, $7,000). For information, call (415) 843-3640.

Important features in *What Next?!* provide information on products "to make your life healthier, safe, and more fun now." Such as:

- Fabrics by Japan's Asahi Chemical Industry Co. that "inhale" the odors from cigarettes and other odor-causing agents. The fabrics, available for the time being only in Japan, can be used in carpets, upholstery, and curtains. (For more information on U.S. roll out, call (212) 736-6890.)
- The Clean Power Washing Disk, a nontoxic alternative to laundry detergents. Put three disks into the washer and electrically charged ceramic particles inside the disks ionize the water as it's being agitated during the wash cycle. This helps release the dirt and odors from clothes. Three reusable disks cost $69 and should last for two years, or five hundred washes (Real

Goods Trading Corp., (800) 762-7325.)

Information on *What Next?!* is available by calling (212) 750-3378. A year's subscription costs $39. The magazine may be available on newsstands in the future.

CHAPTER 9

HUMOR
IN THE NEWS

Life is too serious to be taken seriously.

—Oscar Wilde

Question: What does a grape say when
you step on it?

Answer: Nothing. It just gives you a
little whine.

If you found that nonsense joke funny,
you're probably fairly self-assured and
confident, according to researchers on
how humor affects human behavior.

Let's face it, we all want — and crave
— laughter. Humor is subjective, but
subjective or not, it's *necessary!* And
nowhere is it *more* necessary these days
than in the news. Specifically, I am talking about newspapers. After being
shocked or scared out of our wits by the
daily front page of death, disaster, and
other depressing news, we try for some

relief on the sports pages only to find word of the latest players' strike or drug suspension.

So where can we find the purveyors of pun and cultivators of humor in our newspapers? The comics pages are the icon of humor in the news, and this writer would like to see newspapers run the comics on the front page once a week and put the regular news on the comic page (so we would have a hard time finding *it* for a change!). The next best source of brightness comes from such celebrated humor columnists as Art Buchwald, Dave Barry, Erma Bombeck, and others.

But funny news stories are generally as scarce as hen's teeth in our daily news diet. A sense of humor is a very personal thing, and whether or not a particular story is funny or not often depends on who is reading it. Some would argue that much of the news about our politicians is funny. I laugh every time I think of the possibility of having a president of the United States named Newt, for example. To many people though, who take such things seriously, that would be "Good Newts!"

Finding humorous news stories isn't

easy. I searched newspapers and news on the Internet over a twelve-month period and I was disappointed by the scarcity. There didn't seem to be enough of them to make a chapter devoted to "Humor in the News." But I realized that just because I didn't find more of them, that didn't mean they didn't exist — it just meant that not many of them made their way into our daily newspapers. And that's just another illustration of how the "bad news" crowds out other important information we'd all like to read. Here are the stories I found. I invite you, the readers of this book, to look for more funny stories and send them to me for the next edition of *America's Good News Almanac*. Send your selections to: Bill Bailey, *America's Good News Almanac*, 4363 Hazel Avenue, Suite 1234, Fair Oaks, CA 95628. If your story is selected for the next edition, I will print your name as the source and reward you with an autographed copy of the next edition of *America's Good News Almanac*.

◆ ◆ ◆

If you are a seventy-three-year-old man whose brother is ill and lives 287 miles away, and you want to visit him but have no car and no driver's license, and don't trust trains, planes, or buses, what do you do? From The Laurens Sun *in Iowa comes the funny and poignant tale of:*

The Journey of a Man and His Lawnmower

Laurens, Iowa

Alvin Straight, 73, lives on West Section Line Road in Laurens, Iowa. In late June of 1994 he found out his 80-year-old brother Henry Straight of Blue River, Wisconsin had suffered a slight stroke.

Poor eyesight keeps Alvin from holding a valid driver's license and he doesn't trust anyone else driving for him, and that includes buses, trains or planes . . . so Alvin did the next best thing for him . . . he used his lawnmower.

He had an Arlens riding mower and fixed up a large two-wheel trailer to pull behind the mower. The trailer was licensed but was not equipped with any lights.

Alvin got as far as Emmetsburg (about 25 miles) when his mower gave up. Alvin was brought back to Laurens and he then purchased a 1966 John Deere mower and took off again.

This time he made it to West Bend where this mower gave him some troubles and he spent approximately $250 to get it repaired. This put a strain on Alvin's funds but it didn't stop him. He didn't spend money on motels and restaurants as he camped out along the way using the trailer for sleeping and eating his meals.

Traveling approximately 5 miles per hour for 10 hours a day, Alvin made it to Charles City where he visited a daughter until July 4 when he continued his journey to Blue River, Wisconsin. Rain held back his progress in the Clermont area, and he remained there for some time until his next Social Security check reached him and then he took off again.

Alvin traveled Highway 18 much of the way and anyone who has traveled Highway 18 near the Mississippi River knows that is some road! It stretches your imagination to see how Alvin could have pulled his large trailer with his lawn-mower up and around those hills and could control the trailer and mower as he went down the hills and curves. But as Alvin stated later, "One thing you should know about the Straights, when they make up their mind to do something, they do it!" He said the only time he was stopped by law officers was in Prairie du Chien, Wisconsin, where he was asked to use a side street as he was impeding traffic.

Alvin got within a few miles of the home of his brother when the John Deere mower gave out and he was assisted in getting the mower and trailer to his brother's home by a passerby. He arrived at his brother Henry Straight's, northeast of the village of Mt. Zion, Wisconsin on Monday, August 15. He thought he had traveled about 400 miles as he needed to do some backtracking on Highway 18, but since there is no odometer on the lawnmower, that is only an estimate on miles. This reporter's car registered 287 miles from Alvin's home in Laurens to Henry's home in Blue River by the shortest route he could find.

Apparently Henry recovered from the effects of the stroke, and never knew Alvin was coming to see him until he arrived with his lawnmower.

Alvin Straight's lawnmower trip caught the interest of the national media and Alvin soon was interviewed by Paul Harvey, contacted by the David Letterman and Jay Leno shows (he turned them both down) and was interviewed by newspapers such as *The Washington Post, Milwaukee Sentinel,* and *The Boscobel* (Wisconsin) *Dial,* Associated Press and Gannett News Service.

His trip has made *The Guinness Book of Records,* and the media coverage drew the attention of Paul Condit and his wife in Seminole, Texas. Mrs. Condit suggested to her husband that his Company, The Texas Equipment Co., give Alvin a new lawnmower. Since his company represents John Deere, he quickly agreed, and on September 5, 1994, Alvin received a new $5,000 John Deere Lawn and Garden Tractor from Paul Condit and The Texas Equipment Co. with his old 1966 lawnmower taken in trade. The now famous lawnmower will go on display in Seminole, Texas along with news clippings from the many newspapers that covered Alvin's epic journey.

—By Dar Chaffee
September 8, 1994. Reprinted with permission of *The Laurens Sun* newspaper, Laurens, Iowa.

The following is based on a story from the Associated Press that ran nationwide and was written as seriously as was humanly possible by the reporter. I have rewritten and retitled the story, however, for obvious reasons.

"Good Nudes" for Visiting Teen Athletes

Davie, Florida

A team of teenage baseball players from Venezuela, visiting Florida with their chaperones are staying at a nudist colony.

It's the second year in a row that the team of fourteen- and fifteen-year-olds has stayed at the Seminole Health Club while in Florida for a baseball tournament.

Last year, the team's hotel reservations fell through and all other hotels were booked. A member of the nudist camp works for the tournament host, the George Hickory League International World Series, and the camp put up the team free.

It was an eye-opener for fifteen-year-old Carlos Lovera.

"When the bus would pull into the camp each day, someone on one side of the bus would yell, 'There's one!' and everyone would lunge toward that side of the bus," he said. "And then, 'There's another one!' and we'd all end up on the other side of the bus."

For the eight team members who were here last year, the sight of a naked man strolling by in flip-flops, or a bare-breasted woman making a telephone call, is nothing to get excited about.

"Seen it before," Fernando Busato said with a shrug yesterday as he watched his friends — wearing swim trunks — play Ping-Pong while other teammates splashed in the pool.

Parents of the fifteen team members are not disturbed about the scenery.

"Hey, I was a little concerned last year," said Fernando's mother, Mary Busato, a chaperone for both trips. "He's my son, and being around — well, you know — had me worried. But everyone here is really nice, and no one is DOING anything."

There is actually not much to see at the colony, a collection of small house trailers inhabited by thirty-five permanent residents and, at the moment, two visitors from South Africa.

"Just about everyone stays in their trailers until we give the all clear when the boys leave," said Jan Youngman.

◆ ◆ ◆

Based upon an article by John J. Goldman in the Los Angeles Times *about an upsurge in golf driving ranges in the United States, this story describes an interesting twist that a New York driving range came up with to attract customers.*

Teed Off! Targets New Yorkers Love to Hit!

New York, New York

Maybe there is something inherent in the psyche of New Yorkers that makes it enjoyable to hit David Letterman, Madonna, Donald Trump, and George Steinbrenner on the head with golf balls.

If Sigmund Freud had swung a 5-iron, he might have said it is exercise for the id — that repository of aggressive drives and fantasies residing in us all, particularly in the minds of put-upon, chronically harassed New Yorkers.

In the latest innovation of a burgeoning business, the operators of a New York golf driving range have placed portraits of the show business celebrities, real estate developer, and bellicose New York Yankees team owner as targets to be struck.

At first there was shock.

"Nobody had seen anything like that, and it did create quite a stir," said Berne Finch, assistant manager of the Randalls Island Golf and Family Entertainment Center, just across the East River from Manhattan. "I was a bit apprehensive myself, but it has been pretty well received. I am pleasantly surprised by the way it turned out. I hit at them myself."

Is there something in the personality of New Yorkers that brings added enjoyment to golf when there are targets to hit?

"Oh yes," Finch answered. "I think Madonna is the one most people want to pepper."

Andrew Berkowitz, twenty-six, who works in promotion for Arista Records, held a handful of clubs and said he likes hitting Trump, not Madonna. "Trump does nothing but cause problems for the city," Berkowitz contended.

"I aim straight for David Letterman because he is strategically placed right in front of me," added Hile Jenssen, a Wall Street securities analyst, interrupting swings with her driver. "It means I am hitting it straight . . . I hit him a couple of times."

How did it feel? "Wonderful!"

A private shuttle bus from the East Side of Manhattan runs to the Randalls Island Golf and Entertainment Center, where eight-foot targets of a sultry-eyed Madonna, Letterman smiling with a big cigar, Steinbrenner looking tough, and Trump with a haircut resembling a bird's nest, greet golfers.

Somehow, hitting the caricatures seems appropriate. "They [New Yorkers] are very up-front, very forward, almost brutally truthful," said Finch, who previously worked at a golf course in California. "They will let you know if they don't like something. In California, they will skirt the issue a bit more."

◆ ◆ ◆

Steve Wiegand, a columnist for The Sacramento Bee, *found this story in the police logs, and ran it in his column. It might be called . . .*

Stupid Is As Stupid Does

Sacramento, California

A 53-year-old guy walks into a Sacramento Wells Fargo Bank one summer Friday in 1995 with a note demanding $3,000. The teller is unmoved by the demand, and the would-be robber departs.

The very next day, the same guy comes back with a similar note. Only this time he says he has a bomb in his bag. So the teller tells him to have a seat in the lobby.

And he does. And he sits there right up until the cops are summoned and he is arrested without a struggle. And yes, he had forgotten to bring the bomb. It gets better. According to police, he signed the stickup note "AKA Dr. Lester G. Banks Jr." And the suspect's real name? Lester G. Banks Jr.

—Excerpt from Steve Weigand's column
Copyright, *The Sacramento Bee*,
1995.

♦ ♦ ♦

Our final story comes from Reuters, and

other sources, and though short and seemingly serious, seems an appropriate conclusion to this chapter.

Garbage Men Are Great at Predicting Economy

London, England

Garbage men make better economic forecasters than finance ministers, according to a survey published in the most recent issue of *The Economist* magazine.

In December 1984, the *The Economist* sent a questionnaire to four chairmen of multinational companies, former finance ministers from four countries, four Oxford University students, and four garbage men.

They were asked to predict average economic prospects — including world economic growth, inflation, the price of oil, and the pound's exchange rate against the dollar — in the ten years to 1994.

The Economist said the garbage men and company bosses tied for first with their predictions.

The finance ministers came last.

302

MORE
ACKNOWLEDGMENTS

The stories in this first edition of *America's Good News Almanac* were compiled from many different sources. Some were excerpted from newspapers, magazines, and other periodicals in their entirety, and permissions to reprint were sought and granted by the respective publishers and authors and are listed in the permissions pages of this book. Other stories were provided by volunteer organizations, companies, and individuals. Some news stories prompted this editor to track down the inspiring subjects of the articles, reinterview them, and bring the story as up to date as possible.

All of the stories in this book owe their existence to the reporters, organizations, and publishers who recognized their intrinsic value not as just "good news" stories, but as ones that illustrated the values Americans stand for . . . such as honesty, faith, persistence, and charity, as well as our exceptional sense of humor.

All too often these stories do not get the prominence in our news media they deserve, and I want to acknowledge here the many people who helped me find and compile the *Inspirational True Stories to Warm the Heart* that grace the pages of the first *AMERICA'S GOOD NEWS ALMA-NAC*.

First, my profound thanks to the many permissions people who rushed to fax me last-minute permissions, who are too numerous to list here individually. Peter Goldman, *Newsweek* editor, for his brilliantly written introduction to Chapter 2, "Heroes of All Kinds"; the articles from a commemorative edition of *Newsweek* for the Centennial of the Statue of Liberty was the source of many of our hero selections. To Jean Margaret Smith of Nickelodeon, for her press releases on "The Big Help." To David Boldt, whose recognition of a unique event gave birth to a great story about a very special student. To Art Linkletter, for granting an interview and writing a beautiful endorsement letter for this book. To Hollis Engsley of *USA Today* for his moving story of a man in his eighties who climbed a peak in Antarctica. A special thanks to Donna Dietz, editor of *Positive Living* magazine, and the entire Positive Thinking Foundation and their wonderful annual America's Awards, popularly known as the Nobel Prize of Goodness, for providing me with stories of many of their renowned recipients and other valuable help. To *Caring Magazine* and its publisher for their stories of outstanding Americans.

Thanks to the following persons involved in nonprofit and commercial organizations who helped in gathering information and story ideas. To Kelly Womer, PR director of Hull House Association in Chicago, for the material about Oprah Winfrey's Families for a Better Life Program. To Cheryl Dodwell, publisher of *Who Cares* magazine for her story ideas about young people who care. To Stacy Palmer of the *Chronicle of Philanthropy* newspaper for statistics on charitable contributions in America. To Marilyn Turner and Kathy Meyer of the Business Enterprise Trust for their profiles of corporations with a heart. To Sarah Anderson, formerly of *Caring Magazine*, for her story tip for "Positive Politicians." To Jill Ortman and Reverend Doug Tanner of the Faith and Politics Institute in Washington, D.C., for their contributions to the "Positive Politicians" chapter. To Norm Goldstein for his prompt response to our many permissions requests for stories from Associated Press. To Dr. Paul Klite, founder of the Rocky Mountain Media Watch, for providing the results of its television news report. To Odette Fodor, PR manager for KLM Airlines, for tipping me off to the caring Americans of KLM's unique Bridging the World contest. To the *San Francisco Examiner* for its "Making a Difference" programs.

Finally, to anyone and everyone, including any of you I failed to thank, for your contribution, cooperation, effort, and belief in the importance of these inspiring stories and facts about America and Americans, a heartfelt Thank You! This book would not have been possible without each and every one of you.

The employees of Thorndike Press hope you have enjoyed this Large Print book. All our Large Print titles are designed for easy reading, and all our books are made to last. Other Thorndike Large Print books are available at your library, through selected bookstores, or directly from us.

For information about titles, please call:

(800) 223-2336

To share your comments, please write:

Publisher
Thorndike Press
P.O. Box 159
Thorndike, Maine 04986